RUSSIAN
Myths

THE · LEGENDARY · PAST

RUSSIAN
Myths

ELIZABETH WARNER

THE BRITISH MUSEUM PRESS

Elizabeth Warner has asserted her right to be
identified as the Author of this Work

Published by The British Museum Press
A division of The British Museum Company Ltd
46 Bloomsbury Street, London WC1B 3QQ

A catalogue record for this book is available from
the British Library

ISBN 0 7141 2743 4

Designed by Martin Richards
Cover design by Slatter-Anderson
Set in 10.25 pt Sabon
Printed in Great Britain by Ebenezer Baylis & Son

PICTURE CREDITS
All illustrations were provided by the author
as cited in the captions except those from the
following sources: British Museum (MME
1907.5-20.14) p. 17; John Gilkes p. 6; Russian
Ethnographical Museum, St Petersburg pp. 11,
18, 30, 34, 52, 56, 70.

FRONTISPIECE: *Mikula Selyaninovich
and Prince Vol'ga (see p. 30) illustrated by
I. Bilibin. From* Russkie skazy i byliny
(Leningrad, 1961).

CONTENTS PAGE: *'In the green meadows',
nineteenth-century lithograph illustrating a
folk song. From* Russkii lubok XVII-XIX vv.
(Moscow-Leningrad, 1962).

Contents

Introduction

Russian myth has its roots in a period long before the formation of a distinctively Russian language and culture and shares numerous common features with the mythologies of other Slavonic peoples. The scope of this study, however, precludes any comparative analysis, especially beyond the territories of the East Slavs. It begins at a time when early Slavonic tribes were settling along the river networks between the Baltic and the Black Seas in the seventh and eighth centuries AD. The subsequent impetus for the urbanization and statehood of the early Slavs was provided by the arrival in the ninth century of the Varangians, or Vikings (known locally as the 'Russ'), who were attracted by the commercial advantages offered by this river network, the 'road from the Varangians to the Greeks'. Oleg the Holy established his power base at Ladoga; then, at the head of a predominantly Varangian army he moved south, first to Novgorod and then to Kiev. His seizure of Kiev in 822 led to the foundation of the first Russian state, Kievan Rus. The ruling dynasty soon became slavicized, their Scandinavian names (Oleg) giving way to Slavonic ones (Svyatoslav, Vladimir). The adoption of Christianity in its Oriental-Byzantine form by Vladimir Svyatoslavovich in 988 consolidated princely power and inaugurated a two-hundred year period of political strength and prosperity for Kievan Rus, accompanied by a corresponding flowering of art and culture.

The splitting of the East Slavs into three distinctive cultural and ethnic groups, Russians, Belorussians and Ukrainians came after the breakup of the Kievan state. From the end of the eleventh century the state was fragmenting under the impact of internecine warfare and the constant pressure of Turkic-speaking nomadic groups from the south (notably the Polovtsians). The destruction of Kievan Rus was completed in the thirteenth century with the incursions of the Mongols, the Tartars of Russian epic poetry. Waves of emigration, most significantly to the north-east into what is now central and north Russia, emptied the land. Political power moved to the more northerly cities of Vladimir and Moscow, where eventually modern Russia was gradually established.

'Myth' is a term open to various interpretations. Unlike the Greeks, Indians or Iranians, the Russians have no elaborate corpus of myths about pagan gods, no ancient holy books or extensive epic narratives. However, while the more sophisticated mythological systems may be poorly represented in Russia, the converse is true for the more primitive levels of myth concerned with the natural world, the family and the basic needs of ordinary people. In order to study these we must use the evidence of both folklore and ethnography. This will reveal the presence of mythological themes and *personae* in the beliefs and rituals of everyday life as well as in a variety of literary and artistic forms.

Among the latter are the *bylichki* (sing. *bylichka*), tales mainly about the lesser demigods and spirit-beings, wood demons, water nymphs, spirits of the dead, who populated the familiar universe of the Russian peasantry. This form of memorate, or tale about events that had supposedly taken place in real life and were 'remembered' by the story-teller, shows deeply entrenched patterns of belief about the relationship between the natural and supernatural world in the traditional rural community. *Bylichki* are still being recorded today. The folk tales known as *skazki* (sing. *skazka*), on the other hand, are pure fiction and lack a sacral dimension. Yet here too, especially in the 'wonder' or 'magical' tale (*volshebnaya skazka*), there are mythical layers encrypted in poetic language. It is in the wonder tales that the frightening and enigmatic Baba-Yaga appears. The *byliny* (sing. *bylina*), which mostly relate the exploits of the early heroic defenders of Kievan Rus, blend myth with history, while *legendy* (religious legends) and *dukhovnye stikhi* (sacred verses), in which figures from the Old and New Testaments, saints and hermits meet with ordinary folk, blend myth with Christian piety. The last three forms, in contrast to the *bylichki*, ceased to be part of a living tradition about one hundred years ago. Echoes of myth may be heard in many other folkloric forms. Especially important are spells and incantations, in which Russia is particularly rich. The symbols of mythic thought are woven into traditional embroideries and the carvings that decorate peasant houses. Myth informed both seasonal and family ritual. In other words myth, in one form or another, defines the traditional world-view of the Russians.

Since the systematic collection of Russian folklore and scholarly interest in myth only began in the late eighteenth century, most of the primary sources for this book, both ethnographical and literary, date to the nineteenth and early part of the twentieth century, although many of the aspects of myth discussed here have been documented from the early medieval period and have survived, in one form or another, into our own time.

In this book a transliteration scheme (British Standard 2979: 1958) has been used to represent the Russian (Cyrillic) alphabet. This scheme includes an apostrophe symbol (´) for the Russian 'soft sign', which usually indicates that the preceding consonant is softened. For easier reading of proper names, however, this apostrophe has been replaced by 'y', as in Afanasyev, or omitted, except in the case of Prince Vol'ga where it has been retained in order to distinguish his name from that of the River Volga.

The Pagan Gods

The conversion of Kievan Rus from paganism to Christianity was a slow process, influenced in its earliest stages by the struggles for supremacy between Rus and its powerful Christian neighbour, Byzantium. By the time Prince Vladimir of Kiev, who understood the political and cultural advantages of becoming a Christian, had himself baptized in 988, there were already many Christians in Rus. Some had been converted by Bulgarian missionaries. Others, like the mercenary Varangians in the *druzhina* (bodyguard) of the princes of Kiev, had come under the influence of Greek Orthodoxy while serving in Byzantium. According to the chronicles, the young son of one such Christian Varangian had been chosen by lot in 983 to be sacrificed to the pagan idols in Kiev as a thank-offering for victory in battle.

At the beginning of his reign in 980 Vladimir had not only been a committed pagan himself but had also, possibly by way of providing a counterbalance to the organized, and hence influential, religion of his Christian neighbours, undertaken the task of reforming and systematizing the amorphous cults of the East Slavs. One of his first political statements, therefore, was to erect six idols on a hill just outside his palace in Kiev. The early twelfth-century chronicle

Baptism of Vladimir by the Bishop of Korsun, miniature in the Radziwil chronicle. From Povest' vremennykh let, *pt. 1, ed. V.P. Adrianova-Peretts (Moscow-Leningrad, 1950).*

known as the *Tale of Bygone Years* (*Povest' vremennykh let*) provides the following description:

> There was a wooden idol of Perun, with a silver head and golden moustaches. Then there were Khors, Dazhbog, Stribog, Simargl and Mokosha. People made sacrifices to them, calling them gods, and led their sons and daughters to them. But it was to demons that these sacrifices went and the earth was polluted by them.

These six figures, together with the 'cattle god' (*skotii bog*; cf. *skot*, 'cattle') Volos (or Veles), are regarded as the major deities of the East Slavs.

There is disagreement about the ethnic origins of Vladimir's pantheon, which are clearly not uniform. During the reign of Vladimir the territory of Rus was by no means solely occupied by Slavs. There was a considerable ethnic mix that included Varangians and many tribes of Finno-Ugric and Turkic origin. Peoples of Iranian stock had also passed through the region. Some scholars have considered Khors and Simargl to be of Iranian origin, deriving the former from the Persian word for 'sun'. Others believe Khors to

According to some scholars, this four-sided stone idol found in the mid-nineteenth century near the River Zbrucz in what is now west Ukraine may represent the god Svyantovit, worshipped mainly by Slavs living on the Baltic coast. After A. Gieystor, Mitologia Słowian *(Wydawnictwa Artystyczne i Filmowe, Warsaw, 1982).*

be of Turkic origin. It has been suggested, on the other hand, that Mokosha (or Mokosh) may have Finno-Ugric roots. Dazhbog and Stribog are generally regarded as Slavonic deities.

Many scholarly volumes have been written about the pagan gods of the Slavonic peoples and many elaborate theories constructed in attempts to prove the existence of a sophisticated belief system regulating the relationship between man, nature and the cosmos. However, the actual sources of information on pagan worship among all the Slavs, including those inhabiting the land of Rus, are limited, often contradictory and unreliable. There is some archeological evidence, such as the remains of altars, sanctuaries and sites where idols stood, including the foundations of what might conceivably have been Vladimir's hill-top shrine in Kiev, unearthed by archeologists in 1975. Between the eleventh and early sixteenth centuries, that is well after the Christianization of Rus, there appeared various ecclesiastical texts – sermons and discourses, epistles, questions to be asked during confession, advice on how to live like a Christian and so on – in which the beliefs of the Russians' ancestors as well as the still-lingering remnants of paganism are catalogued and condemned. These include the 'Discourse of one dedicated to Christ, an adherent of the true faith', which was probably written no later than the beginning of the twelfth century, although the oldest extant MS dates to the fourteenth century; and 'The sermon of our holy father Ioann Zlatoust, Archbishop of Constantinople, about how the early pagans believed in idols and brought them offerings', dating to the thirteenth or fourteenth century.

Very influential in forming some idea of Slavonic paganism was 'A commentary on St Gregory's sermon, about how the early pagans, being heathens, worshipped idols and brought them offerings'. The original Greek text, the earliest Slavonic translations of which date to the eleventh century, was a sermon devised by Gregory the Divine for Epiphany. The Russian version contains a number of additions in which the translator comments upon the state of paganism in his own country. Reference is made to the worship of Perun, Khors, Mokosh and Pereplut, the first three of whom were in Vladimir's pantheon. Nothing further is known about the fourth. According to the author, sacrificial offerings were also brought to a variety of mythological beings. These included the *beregini* (cf. *bereg*, 'river bank') and the *vily*, who may be identified as river nymphs, related to the *rusalki* who will be discussed later (pp 42–4). Also mentioned is the worship of fire, personified by the god Svarozhich, and spirits of the dead, including the dangerous *upyri*, forerunners of the vampire

Nineteenth-century clothes 'beetle' from north Russia decorated with protective symbols, including a mermaid or bereginya. *Such implements were used by peasant women for bashing their washing in the river.*

characteristic of later West and South Slav folklore and the *nav'i* in whose honour certain rituals took place in the bath-house.

Small snippets of information may be gleaned from other writings. From the 'Discourse' we learn that the *vily* were regarded by some as goddesses and that the worship of Svarozhich took place 'beneath the drying-barn' (*pod ovinom*), a place where a fire was kept burning in order to dry grain. Here, too, there is a further reference to the cattle god Volos. The Sermon of Ioann Zlatoust comments on the sacrifice of animals, including ritual drowning in propitiation of whatever unclean powers resided in water. The author also deals in more detail with the cult of ancestors, describing how, when the dead were commemorated, ash was spread on the floor to capture their footprints, how meat, milk and eggs were left for them upon the stove and how the bath-house was prepared for them in case they should need to wash. Later, he writes, the untouched food would be eaten by the people who placed it there. In this text, too, the deification of stones is mentioned.

Another aspect of pagan religious observance frequently touched upon by such early commentators concerns the celebratory feasts in honour of Rod and the *rozhanitsy*. Since they are linked etymologically with the notion of family (cf. *rod*, 'clan' or 'kin'; *rozhat'*, 'to give birth'), we may infer that these objects of devotion may have been familial deities. There are also references to places of pagan worship, including groves of sacred trees or huge oaks dedicated to Perun, under which sacrifices were placed.

These and similar texts furnish us with little more than a mythological nomenclature. They must be treated with caution. Neither the historical period nor the ethnic groups to which they refer is ever entirely unambiguous. Authors repeat the matter of their predecessors' texts, such as the names of

BELOW AND OPPOSITE: *Yaroslavna addresses the wind and the sun. Engraving by V. Favorskii from V. Favorskii,* Slovo o polku Igoreve *(Moscow, 1962).*

Vladimir's gods, creating the impression of a greater number of sources than is in fact the case. By the nature of their own religious stance they are naturally distanced from their material and biased. Orthodox missionaries presented their own gloss on East Slav practices just as Catholic missionaries did in respect of the West Slavs.

A different slant on paganism in Kievan Rus is provided by the highly poetic twelfth-century Russian text, the *Lay of Igor's Host* (*Slovo o polku Igoreve*), an account of the ill-fated campaign waged in 1185 by Prince Igor Svyatoslavovich of Novgorod-Seversk against the Polovtsians. This literary work, written some two hundred years after the official conversion of Rus to Christianity, is full of mythological images and allusions. Nature produces one omen after another to warn of the impending slaughter of the men of Rus: a thunderstorm, violent winds, an eclipse of the sun, the cawing of ravens, the howling of wolves and the barking of foxes at the scarlet shields of the warriors as they pass through the gullies. The wind and the sun are appealed to for assistance. Igor's wife Yaroslavna upbraids the sun: 'O bright sun, thrice-bright sun! Warmth and beauty is your gift to all. So why, my lord, have you spread your fiery rays upon the army of my beloved? In the waterless steppe thirst has fettered their bows and anguish sealed up their quivers.' Rivers, such as the friendly Donets and the treacherous Stugna are personified and addressed as if they were living beings. Sorrow is anthropomorphized in the form of a swan-maiden. Of the gods of Vladimir's time the following are mentioned, although without further clarification: Volos, Dazhbog, Stribog and Khors, who is described as 'great'. However, the names are devoid of any devotional connotations, being used in a rather nostalgic way, as if the author were looking back to the dawn of his people. Thus, the people of Rus are 'grandsons of Dazhbog', while the famous bard Boyan the Wise is referred to as the 'grandson of Veles', raising the possibility that Veles/Volos was patron of musicians in addition to being a cattle god.

Perun and Volos

Some of the most reliable and detailed material on the pagan gods may be found in the chronicles of Kievan Rus. Of particular significance for the understanding of paganism in the early history of the Rus state are references to Perun and Volos, the two most prominent deities of the East Slavs. Peace treaties concluded between Rus and Byzantium by the Princes Oleg, Igor and Svyatoslav, in 907, 945 and 971 respectively, show these gods had an important judicial function. The *Tale of Bygone Years* records how in 907 Prince Oleg, with a huge army and a fleet of two thousand ships, set out to capture Constantinople. Finding the city fortified against him, he began a war of attrition in the surrounding area, razing to the ground churches and civilian buildings alike. The peace treaty that followed the Greeks' capitulation was signed and sworn according to the religious custom of both sides, the Christian Greeks kissing the holy cross and the pagan soldiers of Rus swearing an oath upon their weapons, to their god Perun and to Volos.

The name of Perun is linked with that of Volos in two of the three treaties mentioned above. The question then arises: if Volos was so important why did he not have a place in Vladimir's pantheon? The answer may possibly lie in the different functions accorded to the two deities, rather than in their status. Although Perun is generally viewed as the supreme god of the people of Rus, he is also quintessentially a god of war, patron of military leaders and warriors. In 945, when Prince Igor agreed to renew the peace accord with the Greeks, he and his men, in the presence of emissaries from the court of the Emperor Romanus, swore by Perun and laid their weapons and their shields, together with gold, at the base of his idol, in token of their good faith. As the treaties make clear, breaking an oath to Perun would result in an equally warlike vengeance. The oath-breakers would die by their own swords and arrows.

It is likely that Volos, however, is mentioned for a different purpose. The delegations from Rus to the courts of the Byzantine emperors contained many merchants as well as military men and ambassadors, and a major purpose of the treaties was to secure favourable trading terms and conditions. Thus, the

Oleg's campaign against Constantinople in 907, miniature in the Radziwil chronicle. From Povest' vremennykh let, *pt. 1, ed. V.P. Adrianova-Peretts (Moscow-Leningrad, 1950).*

treaty of 907 stipulated the provision of bread, meat, fish, vegetables and wine for traders in Constantinople as well as the building of bath-houses. In the language of Kievan times *skot*, any kind of domestic cattle, also had the secondary meaning of 'riches' or 'money', so that Volos probably functioned as the patron of traders, creators of the wealth of Rus. Although not represented among the state deities outside Vladimir's palace, Volos did have his idol in the merchant quarter of Kiev, down by the River Pochaina, where the trading ships were moored and into which, according to legend, the stone statue of the god was cast after Vladimir's conversion to Christianity.

The cult of Perun was clearly a significant one, long predating Vladimir's time, and had a wide sphere of influence. It was celebrated in other cities of Rus such as Novgorod, where, in the same year Vladimir's pantheon was built in Kiev, his uncle Dobrynya had an idol to Perun placed on the bank of the River Volkhov. Perun was worshipped by the tribes along the Baltic seaboard as well as by the East Slavs. In spite of this, we have few concrete facts about his attributes and functions as a deity. Procopius in his *History of the Gothic Wars* mentions a supreme god worshipped by the Anti and the Slaviny, mercenaries of possible Slav origin, who believed this god to be the creator of lightning and made sacrifices of bulls to him. Some scholars have interpreted this as a reference to Perun. Certainly, from the nineteenth century onwards, it became axiomatic among researchers into Slavonic mythology to regard Perun as a god, not only of war, but also of thunder and lightning, a kind of Slavonic Zeus or Thor, whose weapons were the thunderbolt and the stone hammer. The straight fossils with the pointed ends known as belemnites were, and still are, popularly referred to in Russia as 'thunder arrows' and in Russian folk tradition there has long been an ominous association between weapons such as spears and arrows used in battle and thunder and lightning. A graphic example of this link may be found in the *Lay of Igor's Host* where the impending defeat of Igor's army is heralded by a thunderstorm in which black clouds flicker with blue lightning and rain falls like a shower of arrows.

Apart from several references to Volos as 'cattle god' nothing further is known about him, except that his cult seems to have been particularly observed in the more northerly parts of Rus. There was a stone idol to Volos in Rostov, destroyed, so it was said, by St Avraamii, who had a church built on the spot.

Stribog, Dazhbog and Khors

These three deities are widely believed to have been connected with the worship of air and sun. Stribog, whose name some researchers derive from a Slavonic root for wind, *stri*, is identified in most studies of Slavonic pagan religion as a god of the winds, and Dazhbog and Khors as sun gods. In reality, the evidence relating to Stribog is at best highly ambiguous. It may be found in a passage in the *Lay of Igor's Host* describing the Polovtsian attack on Igor's army: 'The winds, grandsons of Stribog, blow in from the sea with showers of arrows against Igor's valiant host.' The enigma is whether the author is referring to the Slavonic god as the progenitor of the winds – in which case one must wonder why he is sending his arrows, real or metaphorical, to harm a

Prince Igor's army in battle with the Polovtsians. Engraving by V. Favorskii, from V. Favorskii, Slovo o polku Igoreve *(Moscow, 1962).*

Slav army – or whether he is merely parenthetically addressing his audience and using the expression 'grandsons of Stribog' as a generic term, like 'grandsons of Dazhbog' (see p. 13), for his Slav contemporaries.

Khors's claim to be a sun god derives largely from an equally unclear reference in the *Lay*. As far as Dazhbog is concerned, attempts have been made to construct a complex mythology of fire and sun worship around his name, on the basis of little more than a single ambiguous chronicle entry. Under the date 1114 in the *Tale of Bygone Years* the annalist compares the Slavonic deities Dazhbog and Svarog to their Greek equivalents. Dazhbog, son of Svarog, is presented as the sun tsar, known to the Greeks as Helios. Etymologically, the name Dazhbog is probably derived from *bog* ('god') and *davat'/dat'* ('to give'), suggesting that he was a deity who provided munificently for those who worshipped him. He may be related to the Serbian Dabog.

Mokosha and Simargl

Mokosha is usually regarded as a female deity. In spite of the fact that nothing concrete is known about her cult, some Russian scholars have reached the conclusion that she was a goddess of fertility, responsible both for the well-being of crops and for protecting women's work, especially spinning. Deriving her name from *mokryi* ('moist', 'wet'), some researchers link her with the notion of the life-giving moisture of the earth, with the personified Mother Moist-Earth of Russian folklore and with the Christian cult of the Holy Martyr Paraskeva, known in popular tradition as Paraskeva-Pyatnitsa ('Paraskeva Friday'). She was the so-called 'women's saint', patroness of midwifery, water and spinning. On her special day (Friday) there was a taboo against spinning, bathing children and washing clothes. It has been suggested that there is an echo of Mokosha, too, in the female figure characteristic of some Russian embroidery, with her hands raised as if in supplication to the heavens.

North Russian folklore knew a sinister female creature called the *mokosha*. Women who left their unspun yarn at night without first making the sign of the cross over it feared that she would tangle and contaminate it overnight. It was said that the presence in the dark of this creature, who supposedly had a big head and long skinny arms, might be detected by the whirring of her spindle. Although they share the same name, any direct relationship between the *mokosha* and Mokosha is purely hypothetical.

As far as Simargl is concerned, the consensus of opinion is that he is of Iranian origin and may be traced to the fabulous bird of ancient Persia, Senmurv or Simurgh: part bird, part dog, part lion or griffin. In keeping with the Iranian legend that the seeds of plants are disseminated when Senmurv shakes her wings, Vladimir's Simargl is believed to have been a god of crops and vegetation. Some silver bracelets from Kiev and Old Ryzan, dating to the twelfth to thirteenth centuries, show a strange winged creature, sometimes with the paws and head of a dog, sometimes more like a griffin with the head of an eagle, who resembles the engravings of Senmurv on ancient Persian silver and gold dishes. This decoration is thought by some to be a representation of Simargl.

As can easily be seen from the above, facts regarding the higher level of East Slavonic mythology, the deities with political, military, judicial or social significance, are thin on the ground. This has not, however, prevented the elaboration, from the late eighteenth century onwards, of mythological fantasies in which a narrative thread has been teased from the thinnest of materials. In this respect

This late twelfth- or early thirteenth-century silver pendant from a headdress found in Kiev is thought to depict Simargl.

17

the nineteenth-century mythological school, led by A.N. Afanasyev, has played a major role. For the 'mythologists' the worship of nature and elemental forces was the governing factor of Slavonic paganism. Thus for them the sky itself was personified by Svarog, a god of gods, ancestor of the lesser elemental deities and father of heavenly fire in the form of the sun, Dazhbog, and of earthly fire, Svarozhich.

Dual faith

After the official conversion to Christianity, Kiev and its surrounding areas, together with other towns, abandoned the old gods relatively quickly, no doubt seeing the cultural and educational benefits that came with Christianity as well as the obvious political and commercial advantages of joining an ascendant Christendom. Even so, historians recognize a period of approximately two hundred years, from the eleventh to the thirteenth centuries, during which the old faith continued to coexist in some measure with the new, even in higher levels of society and in more sophisticated urban centres. The remoter countryside, however, offers a different story.

Long after the glory of Kiev had waned and the centre of power in the lands of the East Slavs had moved to Muscovy, the isolated hinterlands of Russia continued to manifest in their sacral traditions a unique blending of Christian and pre-Christian beliefs. Both Christian prayers and pagan spells were resorted to for the fulfilling of desires. Magic roots, snake skins and skulls were worn in charms next to the Christian cross. Forest and water demons lived on in the popular imagination alongside angels and cherubim. Major festivals, such as the winter holy days (*svyatki*) between Christmas and Epiphany with their revelries and masking in 'hairy' animal disguises, or Maslenitsa (Butter

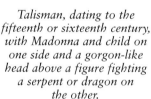

Talisman, dating to the fifteenth or sixteenth century, with Madonna and child on one side and a gorgon-like head above a figure fighting a serpent or dragon on the other.

A personified Maslenitsa (Shrovetide) rides into town with her entourage of jesters, masked revellers and stacks of pancakes. The first pancake of Shrove week was often offered to the souls of the dead. Drawing by A. Bauman from Vsemirnaya Illyustratsiya, *no. 7, 1884.*

Week/Shrovetide) with its bonfires, gluttony and destruction of an effigy of winter, revealed the pagan substratum beneath the Christian surface.

The saints depicted on the Russian icons were referred to as 'gods', a custom denounced by the Church as a remnant of pagan mentality and one that has still not completely died out. Not unnaturally, these saints are among the characters to be found in *legendy* and sacred verses and sometimes also appear, as we shall see, in *byliny* and tales of the supernatural, where they defend mortals against the forces of darkness. In the beliefs and customs of ordinary people the Orthodox saints often contain an extraordinary mixture of Christian and pre-Christian characteristics. We have already noted something of this in the figure of Paraskeva-Pyatnitsa. Paraskeva was envisaged as a young woman with long unbraided hair who travelled the countryside making sure that women observed the interdictions against certain kinds of work on Friday. Her image was confused with that of the 'twelve Fridays', unofficial days of special fasting and devotion also personified in female form by the peasantry. Georgii/George (popularly known as Egorii) was on the one hand 'Egorii the brave', disseminator of Christian values among the heathen and slayer of the demonic dragon, and on the other 'Springtime Egorii', who unlocked the earth after the frosts of winter and protected cattle and horses in the pasture from wild beasts. Paradoxically, he also appears in *bylichki* as an *alter ego* of the wood demon, like him a master of the wolf pack who indicates the sick or wounded animals for the wolves to kill and eat. Only a few Christian saints, however, are explicitly linked with pagan deities.

St Vlasii and the Holy Prophet Ilya (Elijah)

Although most of the pagan gods of Kievan Rus disappeared without trace, an exception might be made for Volos and Perun, who seem to have been reincarnated in the Christian calendar as St Vlasii and the Prophet Ilya respectively.

Vlasii, who is depicted on Russian icons surrounded by cows and sheep, became the patron saint of cattle. His image would be hung in the byre to protect the cattle and his help was invoked when they fell sick. Icons of Vlasii were carried in the ceremonies that marked the spring exodus of cows onto the pastures after the melting of the winter snows. In parts of north Russia his day was celebrated by an abundant feast, and bread blessed by the priest was fed to the cattle.

Perun, god of war and warriors, has long been associated by scholars with the notion of thunderstorms as a sign of his wrath and thunder and lightning as his punitive weapons. On the flimsiest of evidence Afanasyev and his followers reconstructed a myth about Perun as god of war, thunder and fertility in nature. Lightning was interpreted by them as his weapon to dispel the demons of darkness and renew the power of the sun. In the twentieth century this somewhat fanciful theory was expanded by scholars such as V.V. Ivanov and V.N. Toporov, who have postulated the existence of a foundation or primary myth concerning a duel between the thunder-god, representing military interests, and his opponent Volos, representing nature and agriculture.

As the many Russian sayings, beliefs and myths about him testify, Ilya is indubitably connected with the thunderstorm as an instrument of divine retribution. According to the peasants, thunder and lightning were caused by the rumbling of the wheels of his chariot as it hurtled across the skies. He was one of those figures who, like Christ, the Archangel Michael and St Egorii, wielded lightning in a cosmic battle against the Devil, often represented in the form of a dragon. According to folk legend, at the first rumble of thunder heralding Ilya's approach demons scattered in terror and tried to hide: under the caps of toadstools, in trees or stones, in buildings, inside a cow or even a human being. Ilya was immovable in his righteous anger and sent down his lightning shafts against animals and humans alike in his effort to destroy Satan. For this reason, if storm clouds appeared, people would shut themselves up in their houses, pull the curtains over their windows and pray to the prophet for mercy.

However, although the link between Ilya and thunderstorms is clear, any direct connection between Ilya and Perun remains speculative. The profile of Ilya the Thunderer, as he was known, probably owes more to the Old Testament account of the ascent to heaven of Elijah in a chariot of fire and to early Christian moralistic writings in which fiery bolts of lightning are presented as God's weapons against Satan and his minions, than to some atavistic memory of a pagan deity.

The Elements:
Water, Fire, Earth and Air

Water

For Russians, water, fire and earth were, and still are to some extent, regarded as wondrous elements. It was said that all water had a miraculous source. According to the sacred verses about the legendary 'Book of the Dove', which described the creation of man and the natural phenomena of the earth, rivers first burst forth from under a magical stone, the 'father of all stones', 'the white stone called *latyr'*. From there they spread out across the whole world, providing both healing and nourishment. In Russian folklore water may even be closely linked with blood and the life force. The magical 'waters of life and death', for example, can knit together and regenerate a mutilated corpse.

The coming of Christianity did not stop the Russians venerating and making sacrifices to water, which was in a sense the life blood of the early Rus state itself. From the tenth century onwards we find references in a variety of texts to prayers and sacrifices involving rivers, sacred springs and wells. In the so-called 'Law Code of Vladimir Svyatoslavovich', which, according to most researchers, predates the thirteenth-century Mongol invasions of Rus, the misdemeanours deemed more appropriate for an ecclesiastical, rather than a civil court, include 'praying under the drying-barn, in groves and beside water'. Centuries after Russia's official conversion, lists of questions to be answered by the penitent during confession still referred to the deification of springs, wells and lakes, as well as trees, stones and celestial bodies.

Many places of pagan worship beside water eventually became the sites of Christian chapels and shrines and their 'discovery' was attributed to Christian hermits and saints. They were adorned with icons of the Mother of God and both icons and wooden statuettes of St Paraskeva-Pyatnitsa, who, among her other functions, became a patron saint of water. New Christian legends about Russia's great lakes sprang up. The best known of these concerns the submerged city of Kitezh situated on the upper reaches of the Volga. In 1238 the death of Prince Georgii Vsevolodovich at the hands of Batyi, leader of an invading Mongol army, left the city unprotected and at the mercy of the infidels who would undoubtedly have put its Christian inhabitants to the sword and burned its churches. To save the city, so it was said, God caused

Blessing the water at Epiphany in memory of Christ's baptism in the river Jordan.
Any water drawn at Epiphany, blessed or not, was regarded as magical and curative.
Drawing by Tselebrovskii, Niva, no. 1, 1892.

it to sink down into the nearby lake, from where the ringing of church bells and
the voices of the faithful at prayer continued to be heard from under the water.

Water, especially spring water, or 'living water', remained an object of devotion.
In the nineteenth century 'sacrifices' were still being made to whatever spirits lived
there: gifts of scarves and hair-ribbons were tied to nearby trees, and money
and jewellery, even portions of the traditional foods eaten at Easter, Christmas or
New Year, were thrown into wells. Some atavistic memory of human sacrifice
may even be detected in the ritual 'drowning' of anthropomorphic figures. Every
December, for example, on the eve of St Nikolai's day, Nikolai being the patron
saint of sailors and fishermen, a straw effigy was offered up to Lake Onega in
north Russia. The ritual – recorded in the first quarter of the twentieth century
– was conducted by elderly men, one from each fisher family, a sign of the
event's significance for the whole community. The straw effigy was sent out
onto the water in a rickety boat that would be sure to sink with its cargo.

Denizens of the water

We know virtually nothing about the beings to whom the pagan Slavs had
brought their supplications. Later folk narrative, however, portrays a variety of
watery beings. Tales of the supernatural have their spirit-masters, the *vodyanye*
and their female equivalents, the *rusalki*, who will be discussed in the next
chapter. The *skazki* have their water-dwelling dragon, Chudo-Yudo, and their
sea or water tsars in whose underwater realm the young hero is obliged to carry

out a series of impossible tasks, such as the building of a church of pure wax in a single night in order to win the hand of the sea tsar's daughter in marriage. The most vivid incarnation of this ruler of the deep, however, may be found in the *bylina* about Sadko. Uncharacteristically for the *bylina* form this one is not about heroic exploits and has clearly been influenced by folk-tale motifs.

Sadko

Sadko is a poor musician from Novgorod, on the shores of Lake Ilmen. Charmed one day by his playing on the *gusli*, a musical instrument akin to the psaltery, the water tsar encourages him to make a wager with the rich Novgorod merchants that he will catch a golden fish in the lake. Sadko wins his wager,

Sadko by I.E. Repin. The tsar of the sea offers Sadko one of his thirty daughters in marriage. Sadko's saviour St Nikolai warns him to choose the ugliest. Nor should he sleep with her on their wedding night if he wants to escape from the underwater world. From Russkie skazy i byliny *(Leningrad, 1961).*

builds himself a fleet of ships with his winnings and becomes a merchant himself, quickly forgetting his debt of gratitude to the water tsar. Then one day, returning from a successful trading mission, his ships laden with gold, silver and pearls, he finds his fleet becalmed. Sadko proposes the casting of lots to determine which member of his crew should be sacrificed, craftily rigging the process to avoid being thrown overboard himself. But his subterfuge fails and Sadko realizes that his fate is sealed. 'For twelve years I have sailed the sea. I have payed no tribute or dues to the Tsar of the sea. I have not plunged bread and salt into the blue sea of Khvalynsk [a wide stretch of the Volga]. Now death has come to fetch Sadko.' When at last he arrives at the bottom of the sea, Sadko is obliged, as a penance, to play the *gusli* while the water tsar dances, causing disastrous storms in which many ships are lost and Russian sailors drowned. Only the miraculous intervention of St Nikolai, who is upset by this senseless slaughter of Orthodox souls, saves the situation when he instructs Sadko to break the *gusli*'s strings. This *bylina* illustrates the rewards, but also the dangers, of a relationship between human and spirit-beings.

In addition to water-dwelling mythological beings, we find in Russian folklore the notion of water personified. Members of waterside communities, dependant on the water for their livelihood and safety, became intimately acquainted with its moods and vagaries, and made of the water an ally or adversary. Some rivers and lakes were thought of as male, like the Don, who was a bold young hero, others as female, like the Volga, a protective matriarch often referred to affectionately as 'little mother' (*matushka*). These relationships found poetic expression in short folk tales where rivers and lakes interacted with humans and each other, exhibiting human emotions: anger, pity, jealousy. Thus, the Volga and the Vazuza quarrel about which of them arrives first at the 'sea' of Khvalynsk and there are similar tales of rivalry about the Rivers Dnepr and Desna, sons of Lake Ivan, about the Rivers Shat and Don and about the wild and turbulent Sozh and the quiet, leisurely Dnepr, sons of the River Dvina. The symbiotic relationship between man and water in its anthropomorphized form is also highlighted in several *byliny*, such as the following examples.

Sukhman

The *bogatyr'*, or knight, Sukhman, has boasted that he will capture a white swan, alive and unstained by blood, as a gift for Prince Vladimir. In his fruit-less search he travels far, reaching at last the banks of 'Mother Nepra' (a female form of the Dnepr) and sees that there is something amiss with the river, which does not run swift and clear, as it used to do, for its waters are silted up with mud. Nepra speaks to the knight in a human voice, explaining that a horde of Tartars is now encamped on her banks, intent on invading Kiev. Every day they build bridges to cross the river, and every night the river rises in her anger and washes them away. But now Mother Nepra's strength is failing. In this *bylina* not only does the hero relate to the river but, through his tragic death, is himself destined to become one. Single-handed, he takes on the Tartar force, massacring all but three, who lie in wait for him when he returns to the river bank and shoot him with their arrows. When Sukhman returns to Kiev without the promised swan, but with his warnings about the enemy invasion, Prince Vladimir refuses to believe him and throws him into prison. Sukhman is so distraught at this betrayal that he commits suicide, tearing off the bandages of poppy leaves that protect his wounds and allowing his blood to flow free. 'Flow river Sukhman', exclaims the knight, 'from my hot blood, my hot blood, spilt in vain.'

Sukhman is not the only hero in Russian folklore to be transmogrified into a river after death. In the *bylina* about Dunai the same fate befalls the eponymous hero, who marries Nastasya, daughter of the king of the Golden Horde and a renowned warrior in her own right. Determined to prove his own superiority in archery, he arranges a contest between himself and his wife and accidentally kills both her and their unborn child. In his grief and remorse he falls upon his sword. From the bodies of the dead lovers two rivers flow, the Nastasya and the Dunai, now the Russian name for the Danube, although originally it probably just meant a 'big river'.

The young knight and the River Smorodina

In this *bylina* a young knight sets out in search of adventure. Arriving at the banks of the River Smorodina, which had the reputation of being dangerous and ill omened, he asks her advice about how best to cross her swift-flowing currents safely. 'I exact a price,' she warns: 'a Circassian saddle from those who are ferried over, a horse from those who ford the river on horseback, the life of a young knight from those who cross by the bridge.' Nevertheless, recognizing the young man's valour, she allows him to pass unhindered this time. When he reaches the other side, the knight ungratefully makes light of the danger now past and pokes fun at Smorodina, calling her no better than a puddle left by the rain. On his return journey, however, he can find no shallow crossing places and is obliged to force his horse into the deeps. This time the river takes her revenge and drowns the knight, crying out in the voice of a young maiden that pride has been his downfall.

Fire

Although the veneration of water took many more forms among the East Slavs, the sacral connotations of fire were at least as significant.

Fire and the ovin

Some evidence suggests that in the early Middle Ages, in the fire-pit under the floor of the drying-barn either fire itself or the spirit who lived there (*ovinnik*) was still worshipped by the Russians. Until the beginning of the twentieth century in many parts of Russia the beginning and ending of the threshing period (September–November) was marked with a special ceremony. Before the drying process could begin, a new fire had to be lit, and for this event family members and neighbours would gather. The fire was lit in solemn atmosphere, the head of the family bowing reverently towards it. A similar gathering took place when the work was completed and the fire no longer required, an event sometimes referred to as 'the name-day of the *ovin*'. On both occasions food – porridge, pancakes, pies – was shared and also laid by the fire-pit. Sometimes a

This nineteenth-century lithograph of a wedding banquet clearly shows the dominant position of the stove in the peasant interior. Home to the domovoi, *the stove also provided a warm place for children and old people to sleep. From* Russkii lubok XVII-XIX vv. *(Moscow-Leningrad, 1962).*

cockerel was sacrificed, its head and feet being chopped off across the threshold of the *ovin*.

Domestic fire, the stove and the domovoi

The fire within the huge clay or brick-built stove characteristic of central and north Russia was the true heart of the peasant household. According to the old saying, 'the stove is our own dear mother'. New-born babies were placed in contact with it, a betrothed bride sat beside it on the 'wedding' bench. It was linked with notions of good fortune and the well-being of the family. Above all, it was the home of the house-spirit (*domovoi*), guardian of the family and embodiment of ancestral kith and kin.

The stove fire was treated with deference. There was an interdiction against spitting in it, for this was equivalent to 'spitting in the eyes of one's dead ancestors', who might retaliate against such desecration by causing fiery blisters to break out on the offender's tongue and lips. When lighting the fire a respectful demeanour should be maintained and profanities rigorously avoided. 'Tsar-fire burn up for us,' the fire-setter would request, 'not so that we can smoke tobacco, but so that we can cook our porridge.'

Because of its familial significance, it was essential to transfer fire, and the *domovoi* with it, from the old stove to the new when moving house. The fire would be ceremoniously extinguished in the previous domicile and the few remaining embers used in the sober process of re-lighting it. For fear of inviting misfortune, every effort was made in the peasant household both to prevent the fire in the stove from going out and to avoid lending fire to someone else.

Vasilisa the Beautiful and Baba-Yaga

The consequences of flouting the behaviour code in relation to fire are demonstrated in the wonder tale (*volshebnaya skazka*) about the merchant's daughter, Vasilisa. When her mother died, Vasilisa's father remarried, providing her with an archetypal wicked stepmother and two ugly, lazy and jealous step-sisters who persecuted her. One evening the step-mother deliberately doused all fire and light (the same word, *ogon'*, is used for both words in Russian) in the house, leaving a single candle for the girls to work by. When this candle began to gutter, one of the sisters, under the pretext of trimming the wick, extinguished it and Vasilisa was sent to the man-eating ogress, Baba-Yaga, to borrow fire. Vasilisa refused to be intimidated by Baba-Yaga's house, with its fence made out of human bones. Helped by the magic doll inherited from her mother and by her own impeccable behaviour, she managed to survive all the trials devised by Baba-Yaga and was rewarded with the fire she came to seek. This was no ordinary fire, however: it emanated from the glowing eyes of a skull rather than the fiery embers in a clay pot that the young girl would have expected. When Vasilisa returned home she found the house cold and dark, for no one had been able to strike so much as a spark since she left. The skull directed its burning gaze towards the culprits and stared at them until only their charred and blackened remains were left. Thus, Vasilisa's persecutors, who maliciously extinguished fire, also perished by it.

Living fire, tsar fire

It is self-evident that fire is a powerful destructive agency, a fact well appreciated by the forest-dwellers of north Russia, but destruction was not always negative. Fire could also cleanse and purify. In nineteenth-century spells to protect cattle the 'bespeller' threatens 'all wild beasts and unclean spirits with fire and acrid smoke'. As curative fire, it was routinely applied in folk medicine. If some part of the body was diseased or wounded, for example, a cure might be effected by flinging a small clay model of that part into the pure fire of the stove. When

Fire-jumping at the festival of Ivan Kupala in Ukraine. The midsummer bonfires may be a remnant of a sun cult. From Zhivopisnaya Rossiya, *vol. 5, pt. 1, 1897.*

epidemics and cattle plague raged, fire was used in ritual purification ceremonies. Bonfires were built and the sick animals chased through the flames.

Fire could create as well as destroy, a feature that was evident in customs associated with weddings and with couples of marriageable age. Newly-weds would cross over bonfires on their way home from church. At the midsummer festival of Ivan Kupala young men and women would leap high above the flames of bonfires together, hopeful of a forthcoming wedding, should they succeed in holding hands as they landed on the other side.

Fires for ritual protection or purification were lit, not by flint and steel or matches, but by the ancient method of friction on wood. Such fire was known as 'tsar', 'living' or 'wooden' fire. Its sacral nature may be seen in the interdictions surrounding its application. Women were not allowed to create the sacred flame, and this was the one occasion when no other fire must be left alight in the village. Fire in every stove was extinguished in order to be relit with living fire.

Earth

Only slightly less prominent than the veneration of water and fire in East Slavonic mythology was that of earth. However, the quality of the relationship between humans and the earth was somewhat different. Earth (*zemlya*) is a feminine noun in Russian and is a quintessentially feminine concept in Russian and East Slavonic mythology generally. To an agricultural community, in

particular, earth is the moist and fertile provider of crops, into which the seeds of future life are sown. 'A thousand brothers girded with the same belt, placed upright on their mother' is how one riddle describes the harvested sheaves of corn standing upon a field.

There is a strong sense, in Russian beliefs and customs associated with the earth, of a living entity whose good will must be earned and whose feelings must be respected. Those who worked the land

The funeral of Kostroma. The ritual death and burial of figures like this, who were thought to embody the vegetative power of the earth, were frequent in the agrarian calendar and supposedly encouraged the rebirth of crops. Drawing by N. Dmitriev-Orenburgskii, Niva, *no. 48, 1897.*

entered into a delicate personal relationship with it, seeking its blessing before taking what it provided. The sower of the first seed would fast beforehand and sometimes wore the shirt in which he took communion. When the harvests had been gathered in, care was taken to ensure that the generative strength of the earth was preserved for the following year. A gift of bread and salt was offered and the last handful of uncut corn twisted into a plait or 'beard', known as 'Ilya's beard', the ends of which were bent over so that they were in contact with the earth.

It was thought that the earth slept during the winter months, waking and stirring only in the spring when the snows melted and the ground softened. Some even said that the earth was pregnant at this time. It was therefore considered inadvisable to harm it by invasive acts such as ploughing, digging or knocking in stakes for the construction of fences. Only after the spring festival of the Annunciation was such work permitted. Then, the earth began to rouse herself and open up, just as it supposedly closed again on the autumnal festival of the Exaltation of the Cross.

It was not only in the strictly agricultural context that people revealed their belief in the earth's power and sanctity. Well into the nineteenth century a solemn oath sworn upon it was as binding as one sworn to God or upon the Bible. 'May the earth choke me if I act falsely,' peasants would say, placing a lump of earth in their mouth as they paced the boundaries of their fields in order to settle a disputed claim to land. According to popular belief, the earth would not accept the bodies of unrepentant sinners. For the same reason, the earth does not at first absorb the blood of the infernal dragon killed by the knight Dobrynya in the *bylina* 'Dobrynya and the dragon'. There are some versions of the *bylina* in which the dragon's evil continues to work even after its death: 'When Dobrynya killed the accursed dragon, she unleashed her dragon's blood. From the East the blood flowed down towards the West, but Mother Moist-Earth would not consume it.' The resulting flood, which threatens to drown Rus, is only averted when a voice from the heavens instructs the knight to strike his spear against Mother Moist-Earth and command her to 'open wide, in all four directions'.

Ploughing out death

During epidemics affecting humans and cattle a ritual furrow was ploughed around the village. In a reversal of normal agricultural practice the participants in this magical act, whose purpose was the release of the generative and therefore death- and disease-defying forces of the earth, were not men but exclusively women. A woman was harnessed to the plough and another guided the handles. The conduct of the ritual was kept secret from the menfolk and any man unlucky or foolish enough to become mixed up in the action might be severely beaten or even killed.

During the ceremony, the better to interact with the world of the supernatural, the women stripped to their undershirts or even went about naked and barefoot, with their hair loosened from its habitual braids. As they walked, they created as much noise as possible, banging on metal cooking pots and scythes in order to 'flush out' death and disease, imagined as living and

Ritual ploughing led by women from Shemyakino, Kasimov district, Ryazan province, during an outbreak of cattle plague, 1914.

tangible forces which might adopt a human or an animal persona. Sometimes, harmless cats, dogs or hares would fall victim to the frenzy of the chase and if caught were beaten to death. An icon of the Mother of God or of Vlasii, patron saint of cattle and possible descendant of the pagan god Volos, was sometimes carried at the head of the procession, a reminder of the enduring presence of dual faith.

Mikula Selyaninovich and Prince Vol'ga

Among the heroes of the Russian epic poems is one who is distinguished not by great bravery or prowess but by his close ties with the earth. He is Mikula Selyaninovich, the prodigious tiller of the soil who shows that the peaceful agriculturalist can be more successful than the valorous man of war. That he is no ordinary ploughman is evident from the beginning of the *bylina*. Prince Vol'ga, riding to collect tribute from the towns that owe allegiance to him, can hear him far in the distance, whistling as he ploughs, but only on the third day of riding does he catch up with him. Both Mikula himself and the plough he labours with are highly idealized. The curls of the young man's hair are like pearls, his eyes have the brightness of a falcon's and his brows are as black as sable. His boots are of green Morocco leather, with pointed toes, the heels so modishly high a sparrow might fly beneath them. He wears a fur hat and his kaftan is of black velvet. His plough is made of maple wood and has blades of damask steel, a silver mould-board and golden handles. The trial of strength between Prince Vol'ga and Mikula involves the gigantic plough, which must be removed from the furrow and cleared of earth before Mikula can accept the prince's invitation to join his *druzhina*. The combined strength of Vol'ga's army is unable to budge it, whereas Mikula lifts it easily with one hand. Another *bylina* hero, Ilya of Murom, is warned not to engage Mikula in combat for this is a hero 'whom Mother Moist-Earth herself loves'.

Air

Air, in the form of winds, also played a part in the mythologies of the East Slavs. It was thought that winds could hear and respond to human requests. Fishermen in northern Russia would ask the assistance of 'holy air' as they set out to sea, while their wives promised gifts of pancakes and porridge. One of the most emotive poetic images of appeal to the wind may be found in the *Lay of Igor's Host*. Here, Yaroslavna, wife of Price Igor, fearful that her husband has been killed in battle against the Polovtsians, upbraids the wind for assisting the enemies of Rus: 'Wind, oh wind! Why blow, my lord with such strong gusts? Why carry on your light wings the arrows of pagans against the army of my beloved?'

The advantages of appeasing wind above other meteorological phenomena may be seen in the folk tale of the peasant who meets Sun, Wind and Frost on the road. The peasant bows courteously to all three but to Wind he makes a special obeisance. The other two are offended by this distinction. Sun threatens to scorch the peasant and Frost to freeze him. But the Wind can cope with both his rivals. He promises to temper the heat of Sun by blowing cold air. Nor will he permit Frost to harm the peasant, but will blow warm air to counteract his icy breath.

Associated by its very nature with unfettered movement, the wind in folklore is frequently envisaged as a disperser of material and immaterial substances, a feature often exploited for evil purposes. Love spells, for example, sometimes create a powerful sense of elemental forces harnessed in the cause of evil. The unrequited lover may invoke as messengers 'the South wind, the North wind and the winds that sear' and send them to the object of his desire with spells to inflame her heart and bind her to him. Cattle plague, fevers, death itself could travel or be deliberately sent by witchcraft upon the back of the wind.

Destructive winds could be summoned not only by spells and incantations but also by a whistle. In the *bylina* 'Ilya of Murom and Nightingale the Robber' the monstrous opponent of the hero has the ability to harness wind by the power of his voice alone and turns it into a deadly weapon. Ilya, a knight of Holy Rus, sets off from his home town of Murom for Kiev, where, in spite of the great distance between the two locations, he plans to celebrate evening mass. But the shortest road to Kiev turns out to be blocked and overgrown with weeds. The political and religious heart of Rus has been cut off from the rest of its territories by a mythological creature, half-man, half-bird, who lurks near the roadside where it passes through a dangerous quagmire. On the bank of the stream Smorodinka Solovei (Nightingale) has his look-out post in a stout oak, the tree that was once sacred to Perun, from where he challenges the authority of the recently Christianized state, which has also

Ilya of Murom and Nightingale the Robber, nineteenth-century lithograph. From The Lubok: Russian Folk Pictures 17th–19th Century *(Leningrad, 1984).*

marked its territory there with a roadside cross. Although Solovei may have feathers and live in a nest, his voice reveals both his bestial nature and his power of control over the air itself:

> When Solovei begins to whistle with the voice of the nightingale, and to howl, the dog, with the voice of the beast, and to hiss, the accursed one, with the voice of the serpent, then the grasses of the greensward are tangled together, all the azure flowers drop their petals and any humans close at hand lie dead upon the ground.

Later, in Kiev, when Solovei is Ilya's prisoner, he again launches his whistle like a hurricane, shattering windows, killing Prince Vladimir's entourage and forcing the prince to seek shelter under his sable coat.

According to the Russian saying, 'wind is lord, rain provider'. In myth, however, the beneficial aspects of wind are far outweighed by the negative. Of all the elements, air, as storm wind, is the most frequently connected with unclean forces. In folklore wind may be personified as a wanderer, malevolent and unpredictable. In the *skazki*, for example, Veter (Wind) or Vikhr (Whirlwind) replace the dragon as inveterate abductors of females, swooping down from the sky to pluck the tsaritsa or her daughters from the false security of the palace gardens. Inside dust spouts and pillars of snow created by whirling winds little devils run amok, witches and wizards ride to their wedding celebrations, the souls of suicides flee from Satan. Sudden, violent gusts of wind herald the arrival of demonic beings of all kinds, such as Baba-Yaga, a devil or, as we shall see in the next chapter, the wood demon.

Demons and Spirits of Place

U ntil at least the early years of the twentieth century every aspect of the daily lives of the Russian peasantry, down to the most basic activities such as washing and eating, was dominated by an awareness of the ubiquitous presence of spirit-beings, many of whom wished them ill. Collectively, these were known as the 'unclean force' (*nechistaya sila*) or 'unclean ones' (*nechist'*). They were, however, of varying origins, character and function.

Devils and demons

Some aspects of the traditional Russian view of unclean spirits are attributable to the teachings of Christianity and the notion of the struggle between good and evil, disseminated through apocryphal legends, hagiographies, sermons and other Christian literature from Western Europe and Byzantium, as well as from biblical accounts of the fall of Satan. Those devils who entered Russian folk belief from Christian sources eventually became major figures in Russian folk narratives, appearing not only, as one might expect, in *legendy*, which were loosely based on characters and deeds from sacred writings, but also in memorates about the supernatural and in folk tales proper (*skazki*). The folkloric devil inherited from Christianity became a complex and contradictory being. In *legendy* he appears as a tempter of the devout, of hermits in the wilderness and monks in their cells; in folk beliefs he is often presented as the abetter of suicides, those who ended their own life being described as 'a steed for the Devil'; in the *skazki*, where the level of belief in what is narrated is virtually non-existent, the image of the Devil metamorphosed into a comic, even pitiable figure, easily duped and defeated by a more cunning human adversary.

The Orthodox Church, however, lumped under one general condemnatory heading of 'devilish' (*besovskoe*) not only the devils of biblical origin but also the demoted deities of the pre-Christian Slavs, such as Perun and Volos and their idols, as well as the spirit-beings rooted in paganism, who supposedly dwelt in the home and in surrounding nature and continued to loom large in the rural philosophy of the Russians long after the destruction of Vladimir's pantheon had been forgotten. This produced some ambiguities, both in ecclesiastical and in folk literature. In the former one may come across devils whose conduct clearly originates in folk beliefs about pagan spirits of place. The devil who appears to the saint in the 'Life of Saint Evfrosin of Pskov', for example, carries all the hallmarks of the folkloric *leshii*, or demon of the forest. Typically, he first appears in the guise of a peasant known to the saint, and distracts his attention

Heavy is the burden of the sons of Adam. The seven deadly sins in the shape of devils fight the angelic virtues for the soul of man. Folk picture from E.P. Ivanov, Russkii narodnyi lubok *(Leningrad, 1937).*

while leading him ever deeper into the forest, until, at nightfall, the saint awakes from his reverie to find himself poised at the edge of a precipice. Conversely, in folk beliefs and narratives tradition-bearers themselves may use the expression 'devil' (*chort, bes*) as a generic term for unclean spirits of all kinds and may explain the origins of local spirits by reference to apocryphal legends about the fall of Satan, according to which a host of minor demons fell from heaven at the same time as their master. Some remained forever spinning

34

in the air, others dropped straight into the jaws of hell, yet others landed on earth where they quickly found refuge in houses, in the forest, in water and in swamps.

The peasants also gained a good impression of what devils looked like from the images on icons and frescoes, as well as from folk prints (*lubok*) about religious subjects. In appearance, they were small creatures covered in black fur with wings, horns, tails, cloven feet and sharp talons – visual details that sometimes infiltrated the folk perception of local spirits too. In spite of such ambivalence, the functions of local spirits are clearly delineated and separate from those of true fallen angels, suggesting, perhaps, that the former retained a stronger grip on the folk imagination.

Spirits of place

The further north they went, the more difficult and dangerous it became for the ancestors of present-day Russians to establish their small communities along the lake shores and river banks. Agricultural and grazing land had to be torn from the virgin forest and, apart from the actual dangers from wild beasts and winter blizzards, there was, above all, a sense of huge, untamed spaces all around, into which the early settlers were obliged to venture continually – for wood to build or heat their houses, for example, or to hunt and gather the berries and mushrooms that supplemented their diet. This close relationship with elemental nature survived in rural communities down the centuries and helped to shape that sense of divided space – 'one's own' (*svoi*) and 'not one's own' or 'strange' (*chuzhoi*) – which is characteristic of both Russian folk belief and folklore. Scholars have offered various explanations for the spirit 'masters' or 'little tsars', who controlled this natural world.

Afanasyev and the mythological school saw them as mythical personifications of nature, the demoted descendants of ethereal beings, the prime players of long-forgotten myths, whose amours and quarrels were the cause of the rain-showers, thunderstorms, earthquakes and winds that created and destroyed landscapes, changed seasons and made crops grow. Another theory suggested they were minor rustic divinities in a pagan cult of nature, which, unlike Vladimir's higher gods, survived the introduction of Christianity.

Domovoi

The *domovoi* occupied those spaces, namely the *izba* (peasant house) and its adjoining farm buildings, in which the peasants felt most secure. That the home was a protected zone was shown by the careful choice of location for its foundations, in which offerings – bread, coins, wool – were strategically placed; by the sun symbols that often ornamented its facade; by the crosses daubed on door-jambs; and by the stinging nettles hung by windows. In the living area further security was provided by the icon corner and, diagonally opposite, the stove, which, as we saw earlier, was associated with sacral fire and the cult of ancestors. Here lived the *domovoi*, among whose most popular names were 'grandad' and 'master', a spirit-being who shares some features of the household gods of Roman mythology, Lares and Penates. Apart from the stove, the *domovoi* could take up residence in liminal areas between the inner and outer worlds, such as the threshold of the entrance door, the cellar and the attic.

In appearance the *domovoi* could be anthropomorphic or zoomorphic. Commonly, it was said that he resembled a dwarf-like old man, wrinkled and grey-headed, with tangled locks and a shaggy beard that hid his face, apart from a pair of bright eyes, and soft fur that covered his body, including the palms of his hands and the soles of his feet. Hirsuteness was a characteristic feature of demonic beings in general and may be connected with the pictorial representation of devils in icons. The *domovoi* dressed like an ordinary peasant, but usually went barefoot. Sometimes he took on the shape of a cat or dog, frog, rat or other animal. By and large, however, he remained invisible, his presence revealed only by the sounds of rustling and scampering.

The *domovoi*'s main function was and remains, for those who still believe in him, to guard the house, the family, its property and farm animals, whose fertility, health and well-being were his particular concern. At night he busied himself with various tasks in the *izba* and the animal sheds, where his role was inextricably entangled with that of the *dvorovoi* or 'farmyard spirit', ensuring

that everything was clean and tidy and in good repair. He was particularly partial to horses and would groom his favourites, plait their tails and manes, and keep their mangers full of hay. Conversely, he could torment an unfavoured horse by riding it to exhaustion at night. For this reason, the master of the household, when acquiring a new animal, would try to find out which colour his *domovoi* preferred.

Although not by nature wicked, the *domovoi* could also indulge in mischievous games, especially at night, by pinching someone black and blue as they lay asleep, rattling pots and pans or knocking things over. To maintain his good will, therefore, a bowl of porridge or some bread would be left in places he frequented and

A peasant in his holy corner, from where the 'gods' or saints on the icons provided protection for the household. Drawing by Vinogradov, Niva, no. 6, 1891).

Granddad domovoi. *In his role as spirit of the stable the* domovoi *would groom his favourite horses. A careful man would always introduce a newly acquired horse to the* domovoi *and ask him to look after it. Otherwise, the* domovoi *would steal its food and tangle its mane. Drawing by I. Volkov,* Niva, *no. 4, 1891.*

pairs of old bast-sandals hung up for him in the yard. Another duty of the *domovoi* was to read the future and foresee danger ahead. When a family member was awakened in the middle of the night by the touch of a furry hand that was cold and rough, some disaster was likely to occur. If the *domovoi* mimicked the appearance or wore the clothes of the head of the household, that person's death was imminent.

Significantly, it was often said that the *domovoi* resembled the previous master of the household, now deceased, for the *domovoi*'s function extended beyond the immediate family. As an embodiment of the ancestral soul, he provided a link with past generations, and when the family moved to a new house he was always invited to join them: '*Domovoi, domovoi,* don't stay here. Come along with our family.' If, upon taking up residence, the familial spirit encountered a previous *domovoi*, left behind for some reason by strangers, furious battles would erupt between the two rivals. There were even spells designed to protect one from the *domovoi* of others.

Although referred to in early ecclesiastical sources as that 'cursed demon, the house-dweller', the *domovoi* was substantially different from other unclean spirits. He was not afraid of cock-crow, for example, but, most important of all, he resided as of right within the space regarded as 'one's own' by the peasants and his presence there was welcomed, rather than feared.

There were other spirit-beings who dwelt in the spaces between the home and open countryside, the *ovinnik* in the threshing barn and the *polevik* in the field. Beyond the *izby*, close to river or lake, one may still find the bath-houses. These are peripheral structures in every sense of the word, where, at one time, peasant women would give birth, girls were purified before marriage, wizards would be carried to die and spirits were conjured in fortune-telling games. Here, where no icons hang, where fire and water hold sway together, lived the demon of the bath-house, the *bannik*. Those who bathed without his permission, or after midnight, risked death by burning or suffocation.

Leshii

Even today, no Russian living at the forest's edge will take the forest for granted. After a violent storm the most familiar paths can become obliterated and the whole landscape can change. Becoming disoriented and losing one's way were and remain pitfalls faced by all those whose business takes them through the forest. Of all the spaces outside the assimilated territory of the *izba*, the forest most clearly represents the world of 'the other', a territory ruled by the forest demon and entered at one's peril. In the past, peasants would refuse to enter it at night.

The *leshii*, like most spirit-beings from Russian mythology, may look and dress like an ordinary human being. Indeed, he would adopt the appearance of someone familiar to his intended victims in order to induce a false sense of security. Nevertheless, some detail would betray his demonic nature: his kaftan, for example, could be buttoned the wrong way; his eyes might be strangely pale, even white, or he might have no eyebrows; and he cast no shadow and left no footprints. In addition to altering his features, the *leshii* could grow higher than the tree-tops or small enough to hide behind a mushroom or a blade of grass. Many stories about him stress his affinity with the vegetation of the forest. His skin might be gnarled like the bark of a tree, his hair and beard green as grass. The *leshii* could also take the form of animals living in the forest, in particular that of the bear or wolf, with whom he supposedly had a close relationship. He would hoot, roar and howl in the voices of birds and beasts, emit wild bursts of laughter or blood-curdling shrieks and clap his hands loudly. Iconographic influences may be detected in some descriptions of the *leshii*'s appearance, which endow him with a shaggy body, cloven hooves, a tail and horns (golden in the case of the *leshii* 'tsar').

In the forest the *leshii* was master of all flora and fauna and determined the success or failure of the hunt. Since it was necessary to balance the dangers of the forest, both real and imaginary, against the many benefits to be derived from exploiting its riches, rules of behaviour evolved to safeguard those who worked there and to regulate the interaction of humans and spirit-beings. Thus, whistling, swearing, making a noise, wilful damage of flowers or trees, hunting on certain church festivals and so on were discouraged. Protective measures, on the other hand, could be taken against the *leshii*: making the sign of the cross, uttering a prayer or a spell and, more interestingly, reversing one's clothing or retracing one's steps backwards out of the forest. Reversal of the normal, 'back-to-frontness', 'upside-downness', left as opposed to right were all signs of the supernatural in Russian tradition.

The leshii. *These spirit-beings would attack people who broke some law of the forest. They would also fight other* leshie *over territory, causing terrible storms and bringing trees crashing to the ground. Drawing by I.I. Izhakevich,* Niva, *no. 22, 1904.*

There was one aspect of the *leshii*'s behaviour that was connected more than any other with the unpredictable nature of the forest and that the peasants feared greatly. This was his ability to lead both people and animals astray, shifting road-markers and obscuring paths, forcing people to wander in circles until they dropped dead of exhaustion and hunger or fell into a ravine or swamp.

Herdsmen, who, in north Russia even today, allow their cattle to roam freely in search of the small grassy patches of the forest glades, were obliged to develop a pro-active relationship with the forest master. Indeed, as intermediaries between our world and that 'other' world of spirit-beings, their role bordered on the sacral. The imagery of a spell for St Egorii's (George's) day projects a vision of the herdsman, robed in light and girded with a shining raiment, as holy champion of the peasants' 'sweet creatures'. At a crossroads in the forest the herdsman might ask the *leshii* how much it would take to ensure the safe return of his beasts in the evening and would leave gifts there – an egg, especially one dyed red, or a slice of bread sprinkled with salt, the traditional Russian symbol of hospitality.

Far greater than the fear of losing farm animals was that of being abducted oneself. The stealing of unbaptised babies or babies left unattended by mothers working in fields near the forest's edge; the enticing away of little children with nuts and exotic fruits by an old man who looked just like grandad; the kidnapping of young women; an offer to some poor peasant, returning late from market, of a bed in the home of a stranger, who would later draw him to his death in the deepest part of the forest; a drunken peasant returning from the mill, losing his way and drowning in a swamp – such were the typical plots of tales about the *leshii*. The sudden appearances and disappearances of the *leshii* were often associated with high winds. In Archangel province it was said that within the whirlwind the *leshii* danced with his wife. He could ride upon the back of the storm wind, dragging unfortunate passersby with him, and depositing them on the ground again many kilometres from home. No doubt the great speed of movement accredited to the *leshii*, whether on foot or in his troika, may be also traced to this association with wind.

It was said that the *leshii* had a family and lived much like ordinary folk. Many tales about him concern the need to interact with the world of humans from time to time. When his wife was about to give birth, for example, the services of a midwife were required. This need for human company, however, had a darker side. Unlike the *domovoi*, the *leshii* was antagonistic to humans unless persuaded otherwise. He sought human souls to populate his own twilight realm. According to peasant belief, the souls of those who died in the forest without having confessed their sins and received absolution were destined to wander there until the expiry of their own, God-given time on earth. In general, there are many links between the forest, it's spirit master and death. The ancient Slavs buried their dead in groves of trees, a practice that continued into the nineteenth century in respect of suicides and unbaptised babies, often buried in the forest in common graves.

Vodyanoi

The *vodyanoi* was perhaps the most malevolent of the local spirits, his main object being to drown people and animals. No doubt the tales about him performed a useful warning function. Not only fishermen, whose means of livelihood

A water mill on the Donets. Gifts to the demons of the water ensured the miller's safety and prosperity. Drawing from Niva, *no. 31, 1883.*

took them onto the water, ran the risk of drowning. Hunters chasing game in the forest could end up in the embrace of the *bolotnik*, or swamp spirit, a close relative of the *vodyanoi*. Women drawing water in the early morning, or indeed anyone swimming or bathing, were at risk from the *vodyanoi*.

In spring, when rain-storms followed the melting of ice and snow, water became a particularly capricious force, with flash-floods and unexpectedly freezing currents on deceptively warm days. It was at this time of year that the *vodyanoi*, who had remained quiet under the ice between Epiphany and Easter (or until 1 April), awoke hungry and angry. For this reason, bathing was not recommended until after Trinity week. Certain kinds of water, too, were best avoided: mill-streams and mill-races, where little water devils (*vodyanye cherti*) frisked in the droplets splashing from the mill-wheel; and whirlpools and very deep places (*omut*) on rivers and lakes where the *omutnik* lurked, recalling the Russian proverb, 'In still water devils dwell.' One could also expose oneself to the danger of drowning, perhaps entangled in the *vodyanoi*'s fishlike tail, by swimming at unpropitious times of day such as midday, after sunset and midnight, by forgetting to cross oneself or, worse, removing the cross from around one's neck before entering the water.

The *vodyanoi* lived with his wife (*vodyanikha*) and children on the river or lake bed, where he tended his herd of cows, pasturing them at night on meadows close to the river bank. At such times the *vodyanoi* came out onto dry land, presenting a danger to passersby on the river-side paths, and even entering peasant houses. Wherever he went he left damp footprints.

In appearance, the *vodyanoi* resembled a repulsive old man with hirsute body and long, matted hair and beard. It was frequently suggested that, like the devils in Russian icons, he looked black or that his body-hair was black. Some physical details, on the other hand, suggested the influence of the watery milieu in which he lived. Thus, his hair might be green or he might have webbed feet, a fishy tail, scaly skin. Verbal portraits of the *vodyanoi* also frequently revealed his relationship with those who had died by drowning and who provided him with 'family' and 'subjects'. Like theirs, his body would be swollen and bloated, blotchy and bruised, dripping with mud and water weeds, as he rose to the surface. He could change his shape into that of an animal, bird or fish, as well as into inanimate objects, emerging in front of the unwary bather out of some innocent-looking log floating in the water.

Although he might seem a jovial figure, fond of laughter and capable of guaranteeing the fisherman a good catch, in reality his tricks masked a volatile nature. Measures taken to placate him could be extreme and even grisly. In addition to simple and obvious gifts such as vodka or tobacco, animal sacrifices were routinely made to the *vodyanoi*. Fishermen would give him part of the first catch of the season. Chickens, goats and horses, of which the *vodyanoi* was especially fond, were all used as offerings. The masters of water-mills, like fishermen, had to keep in with the water devils, who, when offended or merely enjoying the drunken revelries of a demonic wedding celebration, were capable of causing floods that could breach dams, sweep away mill buildings, open sluice gates or smash mill-wheels. More ominously, the building of a new mill required special precautions in order to avoid loss of human life.

Millers, therefore, took care to ask the *vodyanoi*'s permission, either directly or through the good offices of a wizard, when a new mill was to be built and they would keep him happy by, for example, throwing a horse's skull into the river or sacrificing a black pig.

Rusalka

Of all the spirit-beings linked to specific locations, the *rusalka* is one of the most complex. To some extent, the popular perception of this figure has been diluted by nineteenth-century romantic stories of alluring water nymphs and also no doubt by the sirens of classical literature. The very origin of her name remains unclear, although modern scholarship favours derivation from the ancient Slavonic festival in honour of the dead known as *rusalii*.

By the nineteenth century, scholars had already established that *rusalki* were essentially ghostly creatures, spirits of the dead, rather than water divinities.

The beautiful but deadly rusalka, *with her drowned lovers and children, inspired romantic visual and poetic images. In a poem by Mikhail Lermontov a* rusalka *sings of a dead knight 'asleep' in her river bed home. Like the infant in this picture, he lies 'on a pillow of gleaming sand, by the clustering rushes' shade'. Drawing by I. Volkov,* Niva, *no. 30, 1886.*

For a long time, however, the nature of these dead souls was the subject of debate. Many nineteenth- and early twentieth-century ethnographers were of the opinion that in pre-Christian times any dead person had the potential for becoming a *rusalka*. D.K. Zelenin eventually established that, as the evidence from folk sources clearly indicated, the *rusalki* should be regarded only as unclean dead and specifically as the wraiths of drowned women.

Many of the beliefs and anecdotes concerning the *rusalka* refer to an accidental or violent death, either by suicide or murder, and may be sentimental in nature. The unfortunate ghost, denied the appropriate funeral rites, continues to linger at its place of death, moaning piteously and terrifying those who pass near, or returns to haunt its lost or deceiving lover.

Descriptions of the *rusalki* from all over Russia present them as attractive young women, insubstantial beauties with delicate, pale faces and translucent skin, an indication both of their ghostly nature and of their long residence deep under the waters of river or lake, far from the light of the sun. The *rusalki* often had green hair, like the water weeds and the grasses along the river banks where they frolicked on moonlit nights. Pale blond and even black hair was also common. More significantly, the *rusalka* wore her hair unbraided and uncovered, a state that the Russians associated with the supernatural – witches did not cover their hair either – or with liminality, for a bride's hair was unbraided on the eve of her marriage as was the hair of a dead woman in her coffin. *Rusalki* could also turn into water birds and sometimes had webbed feet. Little information is given about how *rusalki* dressed. Mostly, they went about without clothing or footwear, or wore only a simple white shift without a belt, a detail that, like the loosened hair, supports the notion of the *rusalki* as unclean beings. To the Russian peasantry, going beltless was a violation of civilized Christian behaviour.

While the *domovoi*, *leshii* and *vodyanoi* were all essentially male beings, who occasionally took equivalent female forms or had 'wives', the *rusalki* were unquestionably imagined as female creatures. Their occupations and interests were similar to those of young peasant girls. They enjoyed doing figure dances, singing, giggling and making a deal of noise and chatter. They constructed swings by tying together branches of trees overhanging the water. They could be seen admiring themselves in their mirrors and combing their long hair with magic combs that produced a constant stream of water. They washed their clothes on the river bank and even tried their hand at spinning in order to make garments with which to cover their nakedness.

The *rusalki*'s youth and vulnerability to cold made them objects of pity. Peasant women would hang gifts of cloth, thread or a towel on the branches of trees for them. Yet they were also feared, for their loveless condition turned them into vengeful killers, who seduced young men with their naked charms and the siren-like hypnotism of their songs, or by idly calling out mens' names as they swung in the tree branches. The men who responded were lured into the water and drowned. However, the *rusalki* did not always kill their male victims, reserving their true malice for young women. Sometimes they would merely seize some youth under the armpits and tickle him mercilessly. This activity was so much a part of the *rusalka*'s traditional profile that in some parts of Russia she was known as the 'tickler'. There were tales told, too, of young men who fell in love with a *rusalka* and succeeded in establishing a relationship, even having children, although such liaisons normally ended in tragedy and the death of the babies.

While the *rusalki* of southern Russia, as well as Ukraine and Belorussia (Belarus), had beauty and charm to counterbalance their deadly intentions, there were other parts of the country, particularly the north-east, where the femininity of the *rusalki* was distorted into something grotesque and repulsive. Ancient, haglike creatures with tangled mops of hair, sharp claws and enormous, pendulous bosoms, they seemed to mock all the pleasing attributes of the classic form of the *rusalka*. These hideous beings, who sometimes went under the name of *lobasta*, would snatch travellers from pathways alongside gloomy, marshy places and drag them to a wet and muddy death in their awful embrace.

Although the *rusalki*'s close connection with water is undeniable, their loyalty to and certainly their control over a specific location is much less in evidence than is the case with the *domovoi*, *leshii* or *vodyanoi*. In general, it was thought that during the winter months they remained under the ice-bound rivers but were aroused in spring, when they could climb out onto dry land, remaining there in some cases until autumn. It was believed that during the so-called '*rusalka* week' (the week preceding or following the Orthodox festival of the Holy Trinity [*Troitsa*]) the *rusalki* could be encountered as much on land as in the water, so the peasants would avoid their fields at this time. It was said the *rusalki* particularly favoured fields of flowering rye, and a few sources even suggest they had a beneficial effect on the growth of vegetation. However, there are more indications to the contrary, that the *rusalki*, like witches, were capable of sending inclement weather to devastate a crop.

The emergence of the *rusalki* from the water at Trinity is entirely appropriate. The Saturday before Trinity Sunday was one of those days designated by the Church as an ancestral day on which 'universal requiems' were held for the souls of the dead, and the Thursday of *rusalka* week was traditionally a time for remembrance of the dead who had died prematurely. To ensure the return of the *rusalki* to their homes in the water, ceremonies were held to chase out the *rusalki*. The young girl chosen to impersonate the *rusalka* would lead a procession out into the rye fields, where a noisy and chaotic game would begin, the '*rusalka*' trying to catch people in the crowd in order to tickle them, while the crowd, shouting and banging metal pots, cracking whips, waving brooms and pokers, tried to force the *rusalka* back to the river.

Russian spirits of place are complex, multi-functional beings. On a semantic level the *bylichki* about them illustrate the relationship between the rural Russian and his or her surroundings, from the cosy domesticity of the *izba* to the dark and intimidating forest. In addition to their role as guardians of territories, these mythical beings were also bound up with traditional Russian perceptions of the dead, the *domovoi* embodying the fortunate dead who departed this world from the safety of their homes at the end of a normal life span, while the *vodyanoi*, *rusalka* and *leshii* were related to those who met a premature and violent end in the rivers, swamps and forests, where they remained on the threshold of the world beyond death.

The Dead and the Other World

In any discussion of Russian mythology notions of death and the afterlife or 'other world' (*tot svet*) must play a significant part. The very closeness of the Russians to their dead, their constant acts of commemoration and sharing of food with them, the invocation and propitiation of the dead in agrarian ritual, the role of the *domovoi* and so forth suggest that a cult of the dead was central to their earliest religious consciousness. However, the term 'cult' suggests something both more limited and more coherent than the complex and often contradictory intermingling of pagan and Christian elements typical of later Russian folk religion and folklore. Each folkloric genre, too, has its different themes, 'messages' and bias on the subject.

In general, the traditional world-view of Russians reveals a certain ambivalence about the nature of death as a process, and about its consequences. Nowhere is this more apparent than in the *skazki*, which abound with the oddest notions about life and death: pregnancy occurs through eating a pea; children are generated from a turnip baked in the oven; armies leap into life from a bundle of firewood; animals father or give birth to half-human children. Life destroyed in one form metamorphoses into another: little Ivanushka, murdered by his sister, can still speak with the voice of the reeds growing upon his grave. Death may be reversible: a decapitated dragon can regenerate his heads by touching the stumps with a fiery finger. A person's 'death' can even reside outside their body: the sorcerer Koshchei the Immortal hides his death 'in a duck's egg, inside a duck, inside a hare, inside a box, at the foot of an oak tree, on an island in the middle of the ocean'.

The equivocal nature of death may also be seen in its association with sleep. In the *skazka* about 'Ivan-tsarevich, the Firebird and the Grey Wolf' the mutilated corpse of the tsarevich is revived and made whole when the grey wolf sprinkles the waters of life and death over it. Restored to life again, the tsarevich comments that he has enjoyed 'a long sleep'. In the *bylina* about Sadko the hero enters the other world at the bottom of the ocean by falling asleep on his raft. Being unconscious was also akin to death. It was believed that in this near-death state a person could travel to the other world and still return from there alive. In *legendy*, often as a preview of rewards and punishments to come, the soul thus liberated is led by St Nikolai around heaven and hell to inspect their respective pleasures and torments. Nikolai was regarded, like Peter, as a keeper of the gate to heaven.

The dead who died 'their own' death

Central to the Russians' perception of the dead and what happens to them after death is the concept of a 'good' and a 'bad' death. The former takes place in old age, at the time appointed by God, the dying person surrounded by his or her family. This category of dead is referred to as *roditeli* (lit. 'parents' or 'ancestors'). *Roditeli* were, and are, buried in holy earth after completion of all the rites designed to ensure a safe and swift passage into the afterlife. Their souls depart to face individual judgement before their Maker and are sent for a temporary sojourn to heaven or hell, where their fate may be affected by the prayers of the living. While they await the universal Resurrection and the Last Judgement, these dead are regularly remembered on commemorative occasions at the graveside. *Roditeli* are not expected to haunt the living, either in bodily or spirit form. However, there are exceptions.

According to peasant belief, the corpse remains a sentient being until the committal and should not be upset emotionally or physically. Keening should not begin immediately after the death, since an excessive show of grief might awake the dead. A tear, in the words of a funeral lament, 'can penetrate mother earth, will reach the lid of mother's new coffin, will touch her heart, and my mother will hear her beloved child'.

Merely to wish the dead person alive again is sometimes sufficient to make this happen. The omission of some important part of funeral etiquette, such as reading the Psalter for three days and nights beside the body, as well as inappropriate behaviour towards the dead – burying a man in dirty work clothes, a girl in high-heeled shoes, drinking the vodka for a memorial meal before the event – can also provoke the corpse to rise up again. Such happenings are common in *bylichki* about the dead. Challenging the dead or acting in a blasphemous manner might also have unfortunate consequences. In rural north Russia dressing up as a corpse and performing mock funerals as part of Christmastide mumming games were common until comparatively recently. The 'corpse' was usually played by a youth, dressed in white, with whitened face and vampire-like fangs, but there are also documented cases of a real corpse being used. These and related themes are also aired in *bylichki*, which describe how the dead punish such mischief: a boy who dressed up in a shroud at Christmastide is dragged to a swamp by an angry corpse and abandoned there to the Devil; another, who accepted a dare to shake a corpse's hand, finds himself held in a deadly grip from which he cannot be released.

There are also more elaborate folk-tale versions of similar incidents. In one group of tales a foolhardy young girl boasts that she is afraid of nothing. Egged on by her friends, she removes an icon hanging on the church door and brings it to show them. To make matters worse, returning through the cemetery at dead of night after putting the icon back, she steals the shirt from a corpse sitting on a grave. Naturally, the corpse comes to claim his property, knocking at her window till cock-crow and demanding retribution. Similarly, in tales based on the motif of 'the chopped-off finger' a corpse is outraged and vengeful when a grave-robber or a greedy friend cuts off her fingers and boils them up to acquire her rings.

The dead who died a death 'not their own'

There was another category of dead, greatly feared by the peasants, whose fate was quite different to that of the *roditeli*. These were the people who had died too early. Until the beginning of the twentieth century this category included all who had been murdered or died accidentally, as well as suicides and the victims of epidemics. Since they could not pass into the other world until their

This nineteenth-century copper engraving shows a devil astride a man weighed down by his sins. Suicides, in particular, were called a 'steed for the Devil'. From The Lubok: Russian Folk Pictures 17th–19th Century *(Leningrad, 1984).*

Religious procession through the fields during a drought. Drawing by N. Karazin, Niva, no. 49, 1891.

proper time came, such dead were doomed to remain on earth for the intervening years. The peasants called them *mertvyaki* ('ghouls') or *zalozhnye* (the 'covered up'), possibly a reference to the fact that *zalozhnye* were not buried in the usual manner but flung into ditches or left above ground under a covering of branches, stones and debris. *Zalozhnye* inspired dread and revulsion. It was believed that holy earth would not take their bodies, hence the many *bylichki* about coffins discovered poking out of the ground in spite of repeated burial.

The presence of *roditeli* underground supposedly had a beneficial effect upon the fertility of nature. When the earth warmed up in spring and mild winds blew, the peasants would say 'that is our *roditeli* sighing'. *Zalozhnye*, on the other hand, were accused of causing droughts and hailstorms that destroyed crops. In one nineteenth-century spell against drought from Simbirsk province the bespeller pictures to himself the grave of a drunkard: 'The coffin lies above ground; the earth will not take it ... God's clouds pass it by, no rain falls for seven times twenty versts around this heretic.'

Not all *zalozhnye* necessarily had malevolent intentions. Some returned because of a bond tragically broken by early death: a young man or woman comes to claim a promised marriage partner; friends who have sworn to attend each others weddings 'alive or dead' keep their promise. There are also sad tales about young mothers who have died in childbirth, leaving behind a baby. During the day the infant is not hungry, but at night the father hears the sound of the baby being suckled and rocked in its cradle. Even these well-motivated dead may seem horribly changed – their eyes gleam threateningly, they grind their teeth – and good rarely follows their intervention: the baby dies, the widow visited by her dead husband withers away, the girl claimed by her lover is found lying dead across his grave.

The death of sorcerers, suicides and other great sinners

Among those likely to become *revenants*, or ghosts, were sorcerers and those who had died with many sins upon their souls. It was widely believed that the former made a pact with the Devil and that after death their souls would go straight to hell and pass forever into his keeping. According to folk belief, the death agonies of such evildoers were unusually protracted and violent as demons battled to extract the reluctant souls. In order to ease the anguish of the dying, ways would be found of distracting the demons for a while, by asking them, for example, to recover flax seeds deliberately scattered in a dung heap. The sinful soul and its persecutors were also encouraged to depart by opening the stove-pipe, removing the ninth rafter in the ceiling or by carrying the sorcerer into the bath-house, where the roof would be raised and held open with a branch of aspen. To minimize the risk of joining the 'restless' dead, a sorcerer had to pass on his secret knowledge before death, ideally to a willing apprentice. Even so, devils could reanimate the corpse by crawling in through its mouth or create a zombie from its flayed skin. To discourage this return 'in the flesh', it was said that boiling water should be poured over the cadaver. Cutting the achilles tendons and plunging an aspen stake into the heart of any suspected *revenant* were also recommended.

It goes without saying that any instructions left by a dying sorcerer must be obeyed to the letter. The tale, 'The Heretic Husband and the Brigands', recorded in a village on River Pechora in Archangel province in the 1900s, concerns a peasant who instructs his wife to cense his body for three whole days after his death. Unfortunately, she omits to do this on the third occasion and her 'heretic', that is wizard, husband begins to wake up. Appalled by the sight of the corpse sitting on the bench where he was laid out and sharpening his teeth on a whet-stone, she seeks sanctuary on the stove with her two sons, leaving her daughter behind. First, the wizard devours the baby's swaddling bands abandoned in the cradle, then he eats the little girl. The stove proves an impossible obstacle but he still manages to snatch the baby from its mother. His wife and remaining son are saved when St Egorii, one of those saints whose name was traditionally invoked in spells against sorcery and the evil eye, appears in answer to the widow's prayers, strikes the wizard with his crozier and commands him to descend into the torments of hell.

This *bylichka* reveals the need of *revenants* to eat. The personified figure of death, too, is hungry, as the words of the funeral lament show: 'She came, that evil murderess, cold from the blue sea, hungry from the bare open field.' Time and again, Russian folk narratives suggest that the greatest danger from the walking dead is their appetite for human flesh or, more rarely, blood, hence the tale of the peasant who offers a lift on his cart to a stranger as he drives past a cemetery at dusk. When they reach the village the stranger attempts to enter various houses but finds they are locked against him by the sign of the cross. Only one remains unprotected and here the stranger indulges his blood-lust by extracting a bucketful of blood from the old man and boy who live there.

The other world

Belief in an afterlife and in a place where it could be lived is a major premise of Russian folk beliefs and a common theme in folklore. There is, however, no single, homogeneous definition of the world beyond the grave, even in *legendy* or sacred verses, where the influence of Christian teaching may be felt most strongly. Yet the notion of the journey or road to it is a recurrent image in many folkloric genres, while the Russian expression 'to set off for the other world' is a synonym for 'to die'.

The other world in folk religion

Various aspects of the preparation of a corpse for burial hint at a continued existence of the deceased somewhere, albeit in an altered state. 'Where are you going, dressed up like that?', a daughter asks her father in one nineteenth-century funeral lament. 'Your clothing is not for this world. Your footwear is not like it used to be.'

The coffin was referred to as *domovina* (cf. *dom*, 'house/home') or as the 'new living-room', a 'dark chamber, without windows, without doors'. Until the beginning of the twentieth century this 'domicile' was provided with food and drink, useful or favourite items, such as a handkerchief or a pipe, as well as tools indicating the trade or occupations of the deceased, spinning implements for a woman, an axe for a man. Even today, grave goods still survive in vestigial form. Sweets, water, even a bottle of vodka may be left for the dead person, together with money to pay the ferryman who takes the dead across the fiery river that, according to some beliefs, divides this world from the other, or to buy a billet in the graveyard.

A distant memory of another kind of *domovina*, the underground burial chambers characteristic of East Slav graves around the sixth to eighth centuries AD, may be found in the *bylina* about Mikhailo Potyk, in which the eponymous hero agrees with his sorceress wife that, if one of them should die, the remaining spouse will follow the other into the grave. When his wife Marya White Swan dies, Mikhailo orders the building of a *domovina* of such dimensions that he will be able to stand upright, sit and lie full length. With him he takes provisions of bread and water, candles and incense to last him three months. A possible remnant of these ancient burial structures may be seen in the wooden *domoviny*, not underground but raised on top of grave-sites, that survived in parts of Russia into the twentieth century. These constructions resembled small houses with a roof and a window, through which, some said, the soul could enter and depart at will and food be left for the dead. The simple wooden crosses with 'roofs' that can be seen on poorer graves in rural Russia today may also be regarded as a relic of this kind of graveyard 'home'.

The continued existence of the dead underground is still recognized today through commemorative visits to cemeteries on dates significant to the individual, such as the fortieth day after the death, and on days set aside by the Orthodox Church. In the distant past alcohol was poured directly into the grave-site. Today, a cup or glass may be left upturned on the grave.

Travels of the soul

The Orthodox Church regards the soul as a being of pure spirit whose joys and sufferings are of a spiritual nature, as is its journey heavenwards after death to face individual judgement. In folk religion, on the other hand, the soul was and is envisaged in more concrete terms. Some thought of it as small and childlike.

Toys left on a child's grave at Peredelkino, near Moscow (photo by E. Warner, 1980).

Others said it was a winged creature – fly, moth, butterfly or bird. Funeral laments still abound in bird imagery: a father may be referred to as 'smoke-grey pigeon', and a dead sister is invited to 'take flight like a little bird and come home to your warm nest'. In its winged shape the soul remained on earth for forty days, flying around those places familiar to it in life.

Until the soul left for its final destination, provision was made for its 'bodily' requirements; a glass of vodka placed on a windowsill, a bowl of water and a towel for washing. On the fortieth day the dead person would be invited home. The bath-house would be heated for them, reminding us of the pagan customs denounced by early Christian writers, and a place set at table. After the meal the imagined deceased was accompanied out onto the road leading to the graveyard and told to go to his or her 'own place'. The dead soul's final destination varied and could be reached by walking, crossing water or climbing a steep and slippery mountain. Some even believed the soul flew into the coffin, to dwell with the bodily remains. Wherever it went, it was not expected to return. In funeral laments a barrier of thorn-bushes and stinging nettles – plants normally used to discourage witches and demons – grow on the banks of the river across which the deceased has now passed. The majority of these beliefs and practices can still be encountered today.

The other world in legendy *and sacred verses*

In both these genres the description of the other world is heavily influenced by the heaven and hell of the Bible and other religious texts, together with the elements of judgement, punishment and reward characteristic of these works. The tone of the sacred verses in particular was very moralistic. Here, the souls of the blessed ascend joyfully to the heavenly kingdom, borne aloft on golden salvers by angels or, like the soul of poor Lazarus, whose exaltation is also illustrated in folk prints, nestling on a white shroud. Wicked souls, on the other hand, are cast down into a place of darkness, heat and endless punishment. In sacred verses about the Last Judgement we may read of how Mother Moist-Earth opens with a clap of thunder, disgorging from east to west a river of fire, which bears away the souls of sinners into hell (*ad* or *peklo*), where they are flung into cauldrons of boiling pitch. The river of fire that leads to hell does not always have a subterranean location. The Archangel Michael, serving as

51

Rai, *the fabulous garden where Adam and Eve lived before the Fall and where the souls of the blessed found rest. Folk picture from E.P. Ivanov,* Russkii narodnyi lubok *(Leningrad, 1937).*

boatman, may ferry the good souls over it into the radiant light of paradise, while the bad souls continue onwards into hell.

Images of heaven and hell like the above owe much to popular eschatological literature such as 'The Journey of the Mother of God through the Torments of Hell', the oldest Russian text of which dates to the twelfth century. Such narratives filtered the teaching of the Church down to ordinary people and provided motifs for sacred verses, icons and folk prints. Among the sinners witnessed by the Mother of God are Slav pagans who had refused to abandon the worship of Khors, Volos and Perun, the sun and moon, water and earth.

In both sacred verses and *legendy* paradise (*rai*) is often an upper region associated with the beauties of nature, a wondrous garden through which flow rivers of honey; fragrant flowers, exotic fruits and trees grow there; a multitude of birds sing in sweet voices and gentle beasts roam. For the souls of children there is a heavenly vineyard, where they can pick ripe grapes and golden apples. The purity of heaven may also be symbolized by a well of sweet spring water, whereas the well of hell is polluted by toads and serpents.

Apart from a topography of the other world, which postulates an upper region for good souls and a lower one for bad, we may find in medieval texts, as in Russian folklore, a distribution of souls that allocates the damned to the west and the saved to the east. Thus, in 1489 Gennadii, Archbishop of Novgorod, made a group of condemned heretics ride through the streets, seated backwards on their horses and facing west, towards the fires of hell supposedly prepared for them. Bad souls could also be directed to the left (in Russia, as elsewhere, the side of darkness and the demonic) and good souls to the right.

Late eighteenth-century copper engraving showing the punishment in hell of a money-grubber. Hell takes the shape of a huge dragon's mouth, belching flames. *From* The Lubok: Russian Folk Pictures 17th–19th Century *(Leningrad, 1984).*

Journeys to the other world are a frequent theme of *legendy*. In 'The Soldier and Death' God or Christ gives a soldier the chance to enter paradise in reward for twenty-five years of faithful service in the army, but since neither tobacco nor vodka are permitted there, he chooses hell instead. In 'Brother of Christ' Christ, in the guise of a beggar, invites a young man who was kind to him to visit heaven and hell to see the places set aside for him and his uncharitable mother respectively. In narratives such as these neither ascent nor descent form an essential part of the journey to the other world. The young man walks or rides on a horse sent by Christ. The soldier reaches the Nether Region by taking a left turn in the road or by 'walking near and far, low and high, shallow and deep', a formula traditionally employed in wonder tales. Hell may also be situated in an ordinary *izba* or a large house with many rooms. In one of these, sinners may be punished by cold rather than heat. *Legendy* and sacred verses contain descriptions of both heaven and hell situated across a vast ocean-sea, upon which, according to ancient cosmography, the earth floats.

The other world in the skazki

The wonder tales present their own idiosyncratic picture of a divided world, although the other world there does not appear to be a world of dead souls but rather one of spirit-beings who hold in thrall the still living humans. The action of the tales usually begins: 'In a certain kingdom, in a certain state…' Whether this is or is not Russia is always uncertain, since in individual tales there are indications either way. On the one hand, the villains Baba-Yaga, Koshchei the Immortal and the dragons all detect the presence of the hero because he has 'the smell of Rus' about him. On the other hand, the setting for the tale may be explicitly 'not in our country'. The aim of the tale-tellers was not to provide a realistic picture of some existing land but to transport the listener into a fabulous fairy-tale world. Yet there is no doubting the humanity of the hero of the wonder tale. Whether he be Ivan-tsarevich, Ivan the Fool or even a wondrous youth 'with the sun on his forehead, the moon on the back of his head and stars at the sides', he belongs to the world of the living. Indeed, he (less often she, for a variety of historical and social reasons) could be regarded as a sort of everyman, faced with every kind of existential situation – losing and finding a loved one, danger and death, envy and betrayal, puzzle-solving and striving towards a goal. The tales provide a life-transforming experience for the hero, who returns from his adventures older, wiser and triumphant, as well as a model for the fulfilment of aspirations for the listener.

Firmly embedded in the plot of many *skazki* is the notion of a journey to another location, 'beyond thrice-nine lands, in the thrice-ten kingdom', somewhere beyond the confines of this world. Motivation for this journey is provided either by the need to procure some wondrous object – the apples of youth, healing water, the firebird – or by the tragic incursion of a spirit-being from that other dimension into the normal lives of the main characters. Thus, Koshchei the Immortal, Whirlwind or a dragon may all fly down and steal or, in the case of the last, demand the sacrifice of a human being. Often the victim is the hero's own mother, sister or wife. The journey takes a long time, covers a great distance, is fraught with dangers and the final destination is mysterious. The hero's goal is never referred to as the other world and some researchers have suggested that his travels are no more than an echo of real journeys to exotic foreign lands. Certainly, some tales seem to bear this out. In tales of the type, 'Go I know not whither, bring back I know not what', the hero sets sail upon the seas to fetch ever more wondrous objects for his king and meets with merchants who show him marvels, such as the little box that opens to reveal a beautiful garden.

In fact, there are both similarities and differences between the other world of the dead as depicted in folk beliefs and the countries where the hero of the *skazki* accomplishes his mission. Like the world of the dead, its fantastical location may be high up, on top of a glass or crystal mountain; underground, with its entrance hidden by a rock or a metal slab; 'at the edge of the world, far, far away'; across the ocean; or on the other side of a fiery river or a deep pit. To reach it, the hero requires special directions – from Baba-Yaga, from a silver bird with a golden crest, from a frog carried in a jar of water, for example – or magical objects, such as a ball that rolls in front of him and shows the way. To pass from the human world to the realm of magic, he may require the leap of a wondrous horse, a ride on the back of a monstrous bird, a handkerchief that turns into a bridge, or a rope ladder down which he must climb for three whole years.

The travels of the *skazki* are in some ways reminiscent of visits to the other world in *legendy* and the visions of the unconscious. Here, too, the hero has his guardian angels, his guides and helpers, sees beautiful and terrible things and returns to the real world changed. However, although rewards come to the hero, who learns from his mistakes while evil and treacherous villains come to a sticky end, there is no real moral dimension here, at least in a truly Christian sense, and certainly no suggestion of a heaven and hell. Unlike the virtuous man in the *legenda* 'Brother of Christ', who fails to pull his sinful mother from a vat of boiling pitch in hell, the hero of the tales always succeeds in bringing his mother or bride back from the dragon's lair. If there is any hint of a religious dimension here, it is closer to Siberian shamanism, according to which the shaman in his trance-like state descends to the underworld in order to rescue the souls of those near death.

Some folklorists, following the theories of Vladimir Propp, acknowledge in the travels and trials of the young hero, often the youngest of three or 'of an age to marry', the influence of tribal initiation rites, in which the neophytes, secluded in their initiation hut, may undergo trials that simulate a journey and end with a symbolic death and rebirth into adulthood.

A Siberian shaman drumming to induce a trance (photo by Andris Slapins).

Sorcerers

Magic, its uses and practitioners

Belief in 'magic' and witchcraft is an important strand in the 'lesser' mythologies of the Russians and was endemic in all layers of Russian society until about the end of the eighteenth century, when among the more educated classes rationalism began to take over from the notion of a supernatural providence, divine or otherwise. After that it still remained a dominant principle in the everyday life of the peasantry, in whose world-view the

A healer attempts the cure of a young woman suffering from epilepsy, one of many illnesses believed to be caused by the evil eye, or witchcraft. As the healer says a prayer, she makes the sign of the cross over the woman's head with a knife. Like other metal objects, knives were feared by devils and sorcerers. Uvyaz, Kasimov district, Ryazan province, 1914.

natural and the supernatural spheres were coexistent and interdependent. No misfortune in the natural world happened accidentally but was orchestrated by the forces of good or evil. A drought was not merely a meteorological phenomenon but a punishment from God or the work of a sorcerer. In such a philosophy the practitioners of 'magic', who could manipulate the forces of the natural world by supernatural means, had a crucial role.

All wise folk required some level of occult information and skills. Indeed, 'knowing' is a defining feature of the Russian words for both healer (*znakhar'*, fem. *znakharka*) and witch (*ved'ma*, masc. *vedun*), whose titles are derived from two verbs for 'to know': *znat'* and *vedat'*. Undoubtedly, however, there were some who chose to use their knowledge to cause harm and they became the central figures in beliefs and tales about the exercise of unclean supernatural powers.

Female practitioners of magic: *ved'ma* and *koldun'ya*

Some said that the *ved'ma* originated in the Ukraine and gradually spread from there to 'contaminate' the whole of Russia. Although the term *ved'ma* was not unknown in the north, the negative application of magic there was mostly carried out either by the *koldun* (wizard) or his female *alter ego*, the *koldun'ya*.

There were two types of *ved'ma*. Some were mythical beings with innate gifts passed down the female line. Others learnt their cunning by serving the Devil or by becoming his consort. Alternatively, they inherited their powers from a dying *ved'ma* or undertook a lengthy apprenticeship. More often than not there was little to distinguish the born *ved'ma* physically from ordinary women. Her supernatural provenance might, however, be revealed by a small, furry tail, which grew longer as she matured. Some sources suggest that, like the *koldun*, the *ved'ma* could have two shadows or that, if you looked into her eyes, you would see the world reflected upside down.

In north and south Russia *ved'my* were envisaged differently, and in ways that recall the similar division between northern and southern *rusalki*. In the south they were young, beautiful and seductive, barefoot and scantily dressed, their hair flowing unbraided about their shoulders and immodestly uncovered. At night, with the aid of some magic potion, they would ascend the stove-pipe on their birch-twig besoms, oven-shovels or pokers (phallic symbols in Russian wedding imagery) to attend orgiastic Sabbaths on Bald Mountain near Kiev. Alternatively, they could leave their bodies behind and fly out looking for mischief in the form of butterflies and moths. In the north *ved'my* rarely engaged in Satanic revelry, preferring to congregate at crossroads or on the boundary strips between fields. They were more likely to be old and ugly, hunchbacked or with other deformities and lacking erotic appeal.

Among the features shared by all *ved'my*, *koldun'yi* and *kolduny* was the ability to shape-shift and to transform others. By turning somersaults in some special way, such as 'twelve times across twelve knives', the *ved'ma* could turn herself into a bird, cat, hare or other animal, as well as inanimate objects. In the guise of a pig she would trot about in the dark, tripping up any benighted peasant she encountered and tumbling him to the ground. Among the many

A stereotypical witch with broomstick and black cat betrays the essentially pagan nature of Maslenitsa (Shrovetide) when, according to churchmen, people abandoned themselves to the Devil. Drawing by Karazin, Niva, *no. 8, 1883.*

creatures connected with *ved'my* in beliefs and tales of the supernatural, the magpie occupies a special place. According to one historical legend, Ivan the Terrible, in an effort to eradicate witchcraft from Russia, ordered all suspected witches to be imprisoned in Moscow. A huge pyre of straw was erected in Red Square where they were to be burnt, but as the flames and smoke rose, the witches one after the other turned themselves into magpies and flew away from danger. Throughout Russia it was commonly believed that magpies could harm an unborn child, and pregnant women, therefore, were warned not to leave the house if they heard one twitter.

Some tales about *ved'my* and *koldun'yi* are coloured by Christian notions of the 'demonic' and 'black' arts. The *ved'my* may cohabit with the Devil and carry out his evil deeds by dead of night. The Devil then makes sure that they are never short of provisions and sends his imps to act as handymen.

Ved'mi and *koldun'yi* could cause harm in many ways; by their glances, spells, herbs and roots, by bewitching objects, by sending sickness and death upon the wind, by blowing in someone's mouth or lifting a footprint left in mud. They could affect people's emotions, arousing love or hate against a person's will. There were, however, certain specific activities traditionally linked with sorceresses. These relate to the injuring of cattle, the theft of liquids – in particular milk, but also rain and dew – and to the spoiling of crops.

Many tales about witchcraft among all the East Slavs are concerned with the ways in which *ved'my* and *koldun'yi* contrived to harm cows by stealing their milk. Apart from milking the cow in the normal manner, the sorceress could suck milk from the cow herself or in the shape of some animal, such as a cat or calf; she could milk the cow from a distance into a container which she kept at home; she could draw the milk away to form a puddle somewhere, which she then transfixed with an aspen stake, ensuring that the cow would never give milk again. For fear of witchcraft, in many parts of Russia people were reluctant to lend milk and apprehensive during the buying and selling of cattle. In the past, and still today in places, the peasants protected their animals by drawing crosses on the doors of cattle-sheds, by hanging up bunches of stinging nettles or even a dead magpie.

The peasants would also boil the milk from an afflicted cow or place sharp objects in it, believing that when the witch tried to milk it again she would be burned or cut. In a nineteenth-century *bylichka* from Tula province a prosperous peasant whose cow had inexplicably dried up was advised to keep watch one night in his byre. He was to take an axe with him and hide beneath the chickens' perch. First, a cat came into the byre and began to mew, then it transformed itself into a woman, bareheaded and dressed only in a shift, who began to milk the cow into a leather bag. The peasant struck at her with his axe, using a back-handed blow, and succeeded in striking off her hand. Much to his amazement, the thief turned out to be his own mother, whom he discovered later, moaning and terribly injured.

Sorceresses could collect dew in their aprons at midsummer (during the Ivan Kupala festival) and cause drought by hiding rain away in a pot, in order to release it later as flood or hail. They could appropriate sun, moon and stars. One incantation, whose purpose was to protect from witchcraft, invokes an image of the *ved'ma* as 'a lovely maiden who walked in the forest; herbs she gathered, roots she plucked, the moon she stole, the sun she ate'.

Sorceresses were also accredited with the theft of grain, or indeed any produce of the land. An early reference to this belief may be found in the *Tale of Bygone Years*. In 1071 there was a poor harvest. Two magicians appeared in Rostov province, offering to solve the mystery of the lost crops. From the banks of the Volga they travelled north to settlements on the River Sheksna and Lake Beloozero, everywhere denouncing women from wealthier families and accusing them of hoarding, not only corn but also honey, fish and even furs. Cutting the wretches between the shoulder blades, they would remove by some sleight of hand the stolen goods they claimed to find there and many innocent women perished as a result.

Sometimes beetles or maggots would attack a rye field in flower, leaving behind a pronounced pathway of chewed and damaged stalks. This was known as a *prozhin* (cf. *prozhinat'*, 'to reap a section of field'). Its appearance was also attributed to the work of witches. The witch's 'reaping' differed in subtle ways from that of ordinary folk. She might limit her activity to one special day, such as Ivan Kupala, and preferred working in the dark. She might reap upside down or with special scissors attached to her feet. By this means the sorceress could blight the harvest, taking away its life-force. Later, when her neighbours were cutting or grinding their rye, she would hang a bundle of her illicitly reaped produce in her barn and leave the door ajar, in order to spirit away a part of other people's harvests into her own corn bins.

The wizard: *koldun*

Even in the twenty-first century belief in the ability of some to use magic still lingers in rural communities. The *koldun* is a figure who has always aroused a special awe, combining both respect and fear.

The male *koldun* appears to occupy much the same position in northern Russia as the *ved'ma* does in the south, sharing many of her attributes and carrying out some of the same functions. Some *kolduny* were of supernatural origin, the sons of wizards or the by-product of some unholy coupling between their mother and a devil. Others were cursed by their mother while still in the womb or born under an unlucky star. Yet others served an apprenticeship in sorcery or acquired their knowledge from a dying wizard. Since it was supposedly possible for such a transference to take place without the agreement of the recipient, peasants were wary of accepting gifts or indeed of handling any object, even a cup of water, from the hand of a dying man suspected of sorcery.

In folk beliefs and *bylichki* it may be through the supernatural agency of devils that the *koldun* develops into such a powerful and influential figure. He seeks out devils at their favourite rendezvous, at crossroads, in the bath-house or the drying-barn and agrees to all kinds of blasphemous actions – trampling on an icon, for example – in order to enter their service. To convince the devils of his loyalty, the *koldun* would abjure Christ and every Christian symbol, renounce his parents, even the whole 'wide world' (*belyi svet*) itself. Subsequently, when pronouncing his evil spells, he would explicitly refrain from praying, crossing himself and calling upon the aid of saints and angels, instead invoking the name of Satan.

A more unusual method of shifting allegiance from this world to the other demonic world involved an unholy 'journey' through the open mouth of some animal, such as a dog or a frog. This bizarre rite of passage, or symbolic death and resurrection to a new form of existence, carries echoes of the journey of sinful souls into hell through the gaping jaws of a fearsome dragon, the subject of Russian icons and folk pictures. In the *skazki* the hero or heroine may shape-shift by crawling in one ear of an animal and out the other.

In return for his compliance (commonly involving a document signed in the wizard's blood in the south), it was said that the wizard or 'soul-seller' received all kinds of benefits: the assistance of demons, books of arcane knowledge, wealth without measure. Although the possession of a magic rouble, which could be spent over and over again, was the product of imagination, in the real world *kolduny* were often prosperous because of the gifts they received from clients. Other benefits of the demonic contract were the ability to shape-shift and to become invisible. *Kolduny* were also invulnerable to injury and could only be killed by a brass button.

Whether the *koldun* was of supernatural origin or not, there was often little to distinguish him physically from his neighbours in village society.

Rolling Easter eggs was a favourite pastime of children, but eggs blessed by the priest at the Easter mass were also used in sorcery. Drawing by G. Zeidenberger, Niva, *no. 13, 1895.*

According to many *bylichki* and the accounts of informants, the *koldun* was often of respectable appearance and looked much like any other man. Unlike the *ved'ma*, he rarely possessed a tail although he might have unusual eyes: they reflected objects upside-down or not at all; they were like burning coals; his eyebrows met in the middle; he had no eyelashes; he squinted and so on. There are, however, *bylichki* in which the *koldun* is visualized in a different way. No doubt the traditional representation of demonic figures has contributed to the other common image of the *koldun* as an ancient, surly, dirty and unkempt figure who led a hermit-like existence, wore a shaggy sheepskin coat, had talons in place of fingernails, and long, tangled hair and beard. There were various beliefs associated with the special powers concealed in the wizard's hair. In the Middle Ages it was said that a wizard's head must be shaved before he was put to the torture, as his hair helped him to withstand pain. Among the recommended methods of neutralizing a wizard's power, including knocking his teeth out, drawing blood and biting his nose, was to cut off his beard.

Since people were often anxious to discover whether or not an evil *koldun* was responsible for some misfortune in their lives and since many *kolduny* remained indistinguishable from ordinary folk most of the time, there were many complicated instructions for unmasking them in their true, demonic colours. The best time for doing this was during Lent and Easter week. Thus, wizards might be identified at the Easter mass by taking either the first egg laid by a young hen (Novgorod province) or a painted red egg (Tula province) with you. As the priest intoned 'Christ has arisen' for the first time during the procession around the church, the wizards would be revealed to the holder of the egg with their backs to the altar (and complete with devilish horns).

Weddings

During the transitional phase between the betrothal and consummation of a marriage young couples were at particular risk of 'spoiling' by witchcraft. Clearly, such fears have been around in Russia for a very long time. In 1345, for example, Grand Prince Simeon the Proud sent his new wife Evpraksiya back to her father because, so he said, she had been 'spoiled' and at night seemed to him like a corpse. Care was taken, therefore, during wedding preparations, both to seek the assistance of a friendly wizard and to protect all the participants in the ceremony from the damage that could be inflicted by an unfriendly one. A protective iron fence was raised, in the words of the spell, 'from earth to sky, from east to west, from south to north' around the bride and

The bride bids farewell to her family. The bride's parents stayed behind when she and her groom set off for church. Her father would bless the young couple with an icon, together with bread and salt, symbols of hospitality and well-being, then the path to the waiting sleighs or carts would be swept to remove evil spells. As a further precaution, bride and groom travelled in different vehicles. Drawing by Tselebrovskii, Niva, no. 20, 1891.

groom. Apotropaic magic was used to chase away evil: needles, amber, garlic, onions, salt, the noise of rattles and of metal banging on metal. Avoidance ritual was practised: the wedding train tried not to go over a crossroads, past a cemetery or under a gateway.

Most importantly, the family would invite a *koldun* into their home to purify the house and to remove any evil from the path of the wedding train. Subsequently, the *koldun* would be an honoured guest at the wedding feast. The consequences of not taking these precautions could be serious. An evil-minded or slighted wizard could cause all sorts of trouble. Thus, in a story from Pskov province recorded in 1995 a *koldun* who had not been invited to a certain wedding took his revenge by transfixing the horses so that the party could not set off for the church. The situation was saved by the presence of a second *koldun*. Not only did he remove the hex from the horses but he punished his opponent in a fitting manner by bewitching him where he sat at his window, glaring angrily out at the wedding guests. There he was obliged to remain until everyone returned from the church ceremony. The story is typical in its bewitching of the horses and in its theme of rivalry between two wizards. Another frequent trick of an offended *koldun* was to transform the wedding guests into animals, such as magpies, pigs and most often wolves, poor unfortunate creatures who could live neither as men nor beasts and who were shunned and feared by both. If the bride or groom should fall ill, show indifference towards their new partner or, even worse, give evidence of impotence or frigidity, the blame inevitably fell on the *koldun*.

The 'twist' or 'break' of corn

In general there was a considerable amount of overlap between the functions of *koldun* and *ved'ma*. Both could send *porcha* (lit. 'spoiling', 'harm', 'evil eye'), an ill-defined but tangible entity that could be swallowed, picked up or touched like a contagious disease, and both could affect human relationships, the weather and crops. In the case of the *koldun*, affecting crops was usually achieved by twisting or breaking a handful of stalks in a particular way. The plants would be bent over to the left and then twisted round to the right to form a knot or bundle. In the middle of this objects might be placed – salt, ashes and, most destructive of all, earth taken from a graveyard. The discovery of such a phenomenon caused immediate panic, as all kinds of terrible consequences might follow. On no account should the 'twist' be cut or removed except with the expert advice of another *koldun* or a priest, since a devil sat on every ear of corn. Anyone who cut or ate the grain treated in this way might die. Some said there was no point in reaping the field at all in case the field's owner or his family be harmed by it, others that the yield or the quality would be poor, others again that the life-force of the vegetation had been extracted and transferred elsewhere.

Sorcerers in *byliny*: Marinka and Volkh Vseslavyevich

Although the *skazki* have many sorcerers and enchantresses who pit themselves against the heroes and heroines – deceive and kill a husband, transform the royal children into animals, supplant and traduce the real *tsarevna*, send a whole city to sleep or transform a city into a lake and its inhabitants into fishes – two of the most colourful wielders of magic in Russian folklore may be found in the *byliny*.

The bylina *'Dobrynya and Marinka'*

Many aspects of this and other variants of the *bylina* link Marinka to the sorceresses of folk belief and the *bylichki*: her godlessness (in one version her house is without icons) and alliance with the forces of darkness in the form of a dragon; her use of love spells and 'lifting of footprints'; her loose morals symbolized by the love-birds perched on her windowsill; and of course her ability to change shape. In another version she turns Dobrynya into various creatures associated with witches, including a magpie and a pig.

Some scholars have attempted to find a historical prototype for Marinka in Marina Mnishek, the Polish wife of a renegade monk, Grigorii Otrepyev, who claimed to be Dmitrii the son of Ivan the Terrible. With the help of a Polish army he invaded Muscovy and reigned as tsar from 1605 to 1606. Although there is no evidence to link the *bylina* with historical fact, the real Marina and her husband were both accused of witchcraft, probably because of their alliance with 'heretical', that is Catholic, Poland. Marina could supposedly turn herself into a magpie, and according to the testimony of a Dutchman, Isaac Massa, resident in Moscow at the time, the dead pretender, after his assassination in 1606, was held responsible for the severe and unseasonal frost that destroyed all kinds of vegetation in the vicinity of Moscow.

The action of the *bylina* opens in Kiev. Dobrynya Nikitich, free at last from his onerous duties as Prince Vladimir's chamberlain, sets out in a light-hearted mood for a stroll around the city, taking with him his bow and arrows for pot shots at sparrows, until at last he stands outside the high turret where Marinka dwells. He spies on her windowsill two smoke-grey doves billing and cooing provocatively. Offended at their behaviour, Dobrynya shoots an arrow at them but slips and misses the mark. His arrow smashes through the window, causing considerable damage. Marinka is furious at Dobrynya's uncouth behaviour and takes immediate action to avenge herself. She lifts his footprints from the mud, stokes up her stove with oak logs and casts the sod with the footprint into the flames, pronouncing, as she does so, the words of a love spell: 'As this wood blazes and the young man's footprint with it, so must the heart of young Dobrynya Nikitich catch fire.' Marinka's magic works. Dobrynya's heart is pierced with anguish: he can neither eat nor sleep. Next day he rises as soon as the bells ring for early mass and makes his way to her house, where she is entertaining her lover, the dragon Zmei Gorynych. When Marina refuses to let Dobrynya in, the *bogatyr'* in his fury seizes a huge log of wood to use as a battering-ram and knocks the door off its hinges. The dragon swears at him, calling him a good-for-nothing peasant, but flees with his tail between his legs when Dobrynya draws his sharp sabre and threatens to chop him into tiny pieces, like meat for a pie, and to scatter them over the open steppe. Dobrynya's triumph is short-lived, for Marinka transforms him into an aurochs with golden horns.

For six months nothing more is heard of Dobrynya in Kiev. Then one evening at a royal banquet Marinka, drunk and flirting with the young courtiers, begins to brag about what she has done to him. Also guests at Prince Vladimir's table that night are Dobrynya's mother, the respected widow Afimya Aleksandrovna and her friend Anna Ivanovna who, like Marinka, is a sorceress. Anna Ivanovna does not despair when she hears the news, but boldly walks up to Marinka, slaps her face, knocks her to the ground and begins to stamp upon her white bosom, calling her a bitch and a heretic witch and threatening to turn her into a she-dog so that all the dogs in town will follow after her. Marinka changes herself into a swallow and flies off to the steppe, where she lands on Dobrynya's right horn. She has a proposition. Will Dobrynya, no doubt by now sick of wandering among the fields and marshes, marry her and thus be allowed to resume his human form? Dobrynya agrees and the couple are wed, not according to Christian rites, but by walking three times around a willow bush, in a strange parody of the pagan marriage custom of encircling an oak tree. Now Dobrynya can exercise his authority as husband over Marinka and 'teach her a lesson' for her godless and heretical ways. First, he chops off her hand, for that hand had caressed Zmei Gorynych, then her leg, which had twined itself round that of the dragon, then her mouth and nose, because of the kisses she had given Zmei, and finally her head and tongue, because of her knowledge of spells and witchcraft.

This *bylina* links sorcery and the erotic, and its male dragon, which plays a subsidiary role here, has much in common with the libertine dragons of the wonder tales. In the true heroic *byliny* the villain is a she-dragon (see discussion of dragons below, pp. 68–71).

The bylina *about Volkh Vseslavyevich*

Volkh's name is etymologically linked to *volkhv*, an archaic term for 'wizard'. It is generally accepted that the *bylina* about him is very ancient in origin. Volkh is no selfless crusader-knight of holy Rus, but a shape-shifting magus who uses magic to provision an army, defeat the tsar of India (a country entirely unrelated to any real geographical location) and enrich himself in the process. It is no doubt a reflection of the pre-Christian roots of this *bylina* that no opprobrium is attached to Volkh's mastery of wizardry. On the contrary, his swift acquisition of knowledge is clearly a matter for wonderment and his power over the natural world is used without malevolence.

As in the case of Marinka, scholars have tried to link Volkh with various historical figures, in particular with Prince Vseslav of Polotsk. In 1044, according to the *Tale of Bygone Years*, Vseslav's mother gave birth to him 'with the aid of sorcery'. He was born with a caul, a cap of foetal membrane still covering his head, which was a sign that he might grow up to possess prophetic or other supernatural gifts. However, there is no evidence to link the historical and *bylina* heroes.

The circumstances of Volkh's conception, his father a serpent, his mother human, contain echoes of totemistic beliefs. Walking in the garden one day, the Princess Marfa Vseslavyevna stepped on a snake, which wound itself around her silken stockings and thrashed its tail against her white thighs. Straight away Marfa found she was with child and soon gave birth in Kiev to a wondrous boy. Nature itself proclaimed the miracle: there was an earthquake and a storm at sea; aurochs and deer bounded off beyond the mountains; hares and foxes scurried to the thickets, wolves and bears to the fir-woods, sable and martens to tree-clad hills. Volkh grew with prodigious speed. When only one and a half hours old, he commanded his mother in a voice like thunder to dress him in steel armour instead of scarlet swaddling bands and a silken belt, and to place on his head a golden helmet and in his right hand a heavy mace of lead. By the age of ten he had mastered the cunning art of changing his shape. At fifteen he had an army of seven thousand at his command.

Then Volkh heard a rumour. The tsar of India was preparing to attack Kiev and threatening to raze its fine churches and monasteries to the ground. Volkh decided to take the offensive and set off on the long march to India with his *druzhina*. Along the way he provided his army with clothes and footwear by using his magic powers. At night while they slept, he would leap through the forests in the shape of a grey wolf, killing every kind of animal – hares and foxes, antlered beasts, wolves, bears and, best of all, snow-leopard and sable to make coats for his men. In the shape of a falcon he would fly far off to the blue sea to catch geese and white swans and little grey ducks. Such sweet-tasting food of so many kinds he found for his brave *druzhina*.

Eventually, using his magic again, Volkh penetrates the stronghold of the Indian tsar, where he overhears the tsaritsa telling her husband of her dream about the mighty warrior who had been born in Kiev and who was marching against him. Changing himself into a stoat, the cunning Volkh ran high and low through the palace, gnawing the strings from the tight-strung bows and removing the well-tempered heads from arrows. He tugged out the flints and ramrods from firearms and buried them in the earth. Then he returned for his *druzhina* and marched with them to the walls of the Indian city. The young warriors became despondent when they saw the strong stone walls and the iron gates with their brass locks and bolts, all of which were guarded day and night. At the foot of the gate was a sill of precious walrus tusk, intricately carved in open-work patterns, but only an ant could pass through the tiny gaps. The cunning Volkh changed his men into ants and led them into the Indian kingdom, then he changed them back again into fine young warriors with all their weaponry. The *bylina* ends with Volkh's victory and the division of the spoils, women, cattle, horses, gold and silver from the Indian treasury. Volkh kills the tsar, takes the young tsaritsa for his wife and begins to rule in his place.

Russian folklore knows many different types of sorcerer, some the product of fantasy, others based on real life. Characteristically, and in contrast to Western Europe, little distinction was made in Russia between male and female sorcerers, who were consulted and respected, or condemned and punished more or less equally, although some researchers suggest that a bias against women did develop from the late eighteenth century. Since the Orthodox Church did not share the extremer views of the Latin Church on demonology, Russian sorcerers, in spite of the many tales of their dark powers, were less likely to be accused of devil worship and were largely spared the terrible witch-hunts suffered by their Western, or indeed, Polish counterparts.

Dragons and Baba-Yaga

T he *byliny* contain an esoteric blend of historical detail, which is highly poeticized and often far from accurate, and some remnants of mythological thought. The so-called 'oldest' heroes considered to have mythological roots are the wizard Volkh Vseslavyevich and the giant Svyatogor, who in both *byliny* about him comes to a sticky end – in one case sinking into the ground under the weight of a little bag that contains the earth's gravity, and in the other finding himself trapped in a stone coffin obviously designed for him – suggesting, perhaps, that the time of giants had ended and that heroes of such prodigious size and strength must give way to human *bogatyri*, more suited to the defence of holy Rus. The *byliny* do, of course, have their monsters, such as Nightingale the Robber and the dragon.

The dragon

Dragons play a significant part in the mythologies of many countries. In Russia they occur in most types of folk narrative as well as in some Russian tales of the sixteenth and seventeenth centuries, such as the 'Tale of Petr and Fevroniya of Murom', and in the romance, which may have come to Russia from Persia, about the dragon-slaying knight, Eruslan Lazarevich.

There are also many visual depictions of the dragon. In some folk prints (*lubki*) Eruslan Lazarevich is shown confronting a lake-dwelling creature that resembles a crocodile. In others the dragon is a winged, scaly monster, with sharp claws, a long, coiling tail and three or six heads, which are either crested or crowned. It has a barbed tongue and its tail too may be barbed or tufted. Moralistic folk pictures showing the temptation, fall and torments of sinners, together with icons and frescoes of the Last Judgement, have clearly been influenced by the 'Revelation of John', where the dragon, 'that ancient serpent, who is the Devil and Satan', is tossed out of heaven into a bottomless pit. In these illustrations the chthonic or subterranean persona of the dragon is more often emphasized, as he tortures the damned in fiery, underground caverns. Frequently, the dragon becomes a mere metaphor for the gates of hell and is reduced to a fire-belching, gaping maw situated at the foot of the picture, into whose flames the condemned sinners tumble down.

The battle between St Egorii and the dragon is depicted on Russian icons, too. In some, such as the one illustrated on the front cover of this book, the saint is shown plunging his spear into the dragon. This scene can be found in a large number of icons dating to the twelfth to eighteenth centuries. In others, which

Eruslan fights the dragon from the lake. Nineteenth-century lithograph from Russkii lubok XVII-XIX vv. *(Leningrad, 1962).*

are much rarer, the saint follows behind Elizaveta, the maiden he has rescued, who leads the defeated dragon like a dog on a leash. This particular subject echoes the sacred verses about 'Egorii the Brave and Elizaveta the Beautiful', which tells the story of a pagan land scourged by a man-eating dragon sent by God as a punishment. The time comes for Elizaveta, the Christian daughter of the tsar, to be eaten but she is saved by Egorii, a soldier riding by on his white horse.

The dragons of Russian folklore may be either male (*zmei*) or female (*zmeya*), a gender difference that affects the motivation and actions of the dragons themselves as well as their relationship with the heroes. The dragon at the heart of the *byliny* is female, whereas in the *skazki* it is usually male, except in the case where a vengeful mother dragon pursues the hero who has destroyed her sons.

The dragon in byliny

In the Kievan cycle of *byliny*, which dates to the tenth to fourteenth centuries and deals with the heroic defence of Kievan Rus against its external enemies, the dragon-slayer is Dobrynya Nikitich, often identified with the historical figure of Dobrynya who lived in the second half of the tenth century and was uncle to Vladimir I of Kiev.

The *bylina* about Dobrynya's fight with the dragon was a popular one, existing in more than one hundred versions. It usually begins with a parental warning. Dobrynya's mother forbids him to go bathing in the dangerous River

Puchai, home to a fierce dragon. Dobrynya defies his mother, rides a long distance to the river and leaps, naked, into its waves. The dragon appears and attacks the defenceless hero. Dobrynya seizes the first 'weapon' he can reach, his 'hat from the Greek land' lying on the river bank. He defeats the dragon and concludes a bargain with her – she will stop flying into Rus and he will spare her life. However, the perfidious dragon breaks her word and kidnaps Vladimir's own niece (or daughter), Zabava. Dobrynya is then given the task of rescuing her. He hunts down the dragon and goes into battle with her a second time, overcoming her at last with the help of magic objects from his mother, a silken whip with which to beat his horse when its strength flags and a silken handkerchief to wipe his own face. When the dragon is dead, Dobrynya finds her mountain lair, where he kills a nest of baby dragons and releases Zabava and the other inhabitants of Rus held captive by the dragon. In addition to mountains, the dragon (in folk tales as well as *byliny*) is associated with water and fire. The River Puchai, which marks the boundary of her territory, belches smoke and flames and has a swift, 'scalding' current. The dragon also breathes fire and showers Dobrynya with sparks.

The role of the epic dragon may be interpreted in different ways. On the one hand, she is an unclean demonic creature, who, like other spirit-beings, inhabits a distant other world beyond the fiery river. The *byliny*, however, contain historical as well as fantastic elements. Dobrynya's fight with the dragon was conceived in the period of dual faith when Christianity was still struggling against the monsters of paganism. It is not difficult, therefore, to envisage the dragon as a symbol of paganism and Dobrynya as the champion of Christendom. Some scholars have suggested that the River Puchai is a distortion of the Pochaina, a river near Kiev, in which, according to legend, the citizens of Kiev were forcibly baptized in 988. In such a context the enigmatic 'hat from the Greek land' with which Dobrynya strikes his enemy has been interpreted as a symbol of Christianity. This is no ordinary hat, then, but the characteristic headgear inherited from the 'Greek land', that is Byzantium, worn by priests of the Orthodox Church and sometimes by pilgrims who had visited the Holy Land.

Dobrynya is certainly a knight of Holy Rus. Before engaging battle he may pray to St Mikola (Nikolai) and ask the Lord, his Saviour, to have mercy upon him. As we saw earlier (p. 29), he is saved from drowning in the dragon's blood by divine intervention. The epic dragon is bound up with the historical fate of Kievan Rus and with its defence against foes, such as the nomadic Polovtsians who swept across the southern steppe-lands in the eleventh to twelfth centuries or the Tartar-Mongol hordes who ravaged Rus in the thirteenth century, sacking Kiev and destroying its glory. Dobrynya is a *bogatyr'* in the elite bodyguard of Prince Vladimir of Kiev. His fine steed, its accoutrements (the tasselled bridle, the Circassian saddle) and his weapons (taut bow and well-fired arrows, sharp sabre, long spear and cudgel) are described in loving detail. Much in the behaviour of the dragon might be a reflection of the pagan Polovtsians and other steppe nomads: the unexpected raids, the rustling of cattle and the seizure of prisoners as slaves and concubines. The chronicles refer to the Polovtsians as oath-breakers and 'serpents'. The description of the dragon's lair deep in the mountain is reminiscent of a medieval dungeon or torture chamber. In one text

In this nineteenth-century print denouncing drunkenness and its evil consequences the blood of the dragon, Satan, is vodka.

the princess whom Dobrynya has been sent to save has been crucified against a wall, with iron nails hammered into her hands and feet.

In the *byliny* about Dobrynya a female dragon is pitted against a male hero, who kills her babies and threatens the continued existence of her race. Although there is nothing overtly sexual in their encounter, there are hints in some versions that the dragon's female prisoners are there to service her male children, either as wet-nurses or as marriage partners. In one variant the captive princess sings a wedding lament in which she mentions the 'little serpents who will unwind my braid', a reference to the traditional loosening of a bride's plaited hair in preparation for her wedding day.

The dragon in the wonder tale

The villainous deeds of the folk-tale dragon include killing and eating both people and cattle, scorching grass and crops, stealing water and daylight, causing droughts and generally laying waste to the lands he invades. One activity above all, however, defines his function in the tales: the kidnapping, requisitioning or seduction of women, who are destined to be eaten or become his paramours.

In the *byliny* the dragon is a marauder whose activities threaten the integrity of the Kievan state and Dobrynya opposes her as an enemy of his country. He neither seeks, nor gains a marriage partner as a result of his freeing of Zabava from her clutches. In the *skazki* similar mythological elements are presented in terms of the hero's personal quest for fulfilment and the solution of existential problems, in which the search for a bride plays a major role. Courtship, in other words, is a prime mover of the action in the wonder tales. In some cases the dragon can even become the hero's direct rival: as a male predator *par excellence*, he courts or kidnaps potential marriage partners of the hero and may even corrupt the hero's wife once he is married. Otherwise he may kidnap the hero's mother or sister, providing another very personal motive for revenge.

Although there is some overlapping from one tale to another, one can identify several groups of tales that are strongly bound up with the dragon motif. These include 'The Three Kingdoms of Bronze, Silver and Gold', 'Pokatigoroshek' ('Rolling Pea') and tales about Ivan Popyalov (Ivan Cinders) or three heroic comrades whose mothers are impregnated simultaneously from a single magical source. Thus, in the tale of Ivan Bykovich (Ivan, Son of Bull) the tsar's wife, a kitchen maid and a cow all conceive after eating parts of the 'ruff [perch] with the golden scales'. One might also mention tales about two brothers, such as the two Ivans (sons of a soldier), and 'Milk of Beasts'.

Each type of tale reveals some slightly different aspects of the dragon. In tales about the three kingdoms the dragon is a kidnapper who flies off with Ivan-tsarevich's mother, Nastasya of the Golden Braid. Here, as in the *byliny*, the dragon is linked with mountains. In one particular version of the tale Ivan-tsarevich, seeking his mother, comes to a mountain range so high there seems no way of reaching the top. But the tsarevich whips his horse into a fury so that it leaps 'higher than the standing forest, lower than the scudding clouds' and lands on the summit. Up here, the dragons with three, six, nine and twelve heads have their palaces. In the diamond palace, which revolves like a windmill and from which the whole universe is visible, 'all kingdoms and lands spread out as if on the palm of one's hand', Ivan finds his mother. The tales about Pokatigoroshek are mainly Ukrainian and Belorussian. They concern the rescue from the dragon of a brother and sister by the youngest member of their family, the young ploughman Pokatigoroshek, conceived when his mother swallowed a pea. In tales of two brothers the central episode usually involves a sea-dragon that threatens to devastate the whole country unless it receives tribute in the form of a regular supply of young women. In 'Milk of Beasts' the dragon is a sly seducer who conspires with the wife of Prince Ivan to rid her of her husband.

One of the most interesting folk tales about dragons is the tale of Ivan Bykovich and his 'brothers', which contains the famous episode of the battle on the bridge of guelder-rose wood across the fiery River Smorodina, linking two inimical worlds. This story differs from the others in that the heroes themselves, without any prior provocation, deliberately set off to find the dragon and engage it in mortal combat. On their way they receive guidance from the ogress Baba-Yaga who informs them how the dragons have brought ruin to the whole country. Indeed, they soon find this out for themselves, for when they reach the rose-wood bridge, across which the dragons ride to attack the world of mortal men, they see the piles of skulls and human bones piled up on the river bank. The three dragons fought by Ivan Bykovich, each progressively larger and stronger than the preceding one, have a number of characteristic features. These dragons do not fly but have winged horses. The twelve-headed dragon has a horse with twelve wings, a coat of silver and a tail and mane of gold. In another variant the horse is black with a golden moon emblazoned on its forehead and clusters of stars upon its flanks. These attributes carry echoes of the three kingdoms of the other world, of the dragons' treasure troves deep in the mountains and of the night sky.

In *byliny* and folk tales alike dragons are portrayed as elemental creatures in close touch with water, fire and air and the darker forces of nature. At their approach eagles scream from the tops of oak trees, lightning flashes, thunder roars and blustery winds whip up waves on river and sea.

Dragons in smithing and ploughing

Two episodes encountered in folk tales about dragons may be the remnants of culture myths. In the first the main hero, whether he be Pokatigoroshek, Ivan Popyalov or Storm Warrior, Son of a Cow, finds himself on the run from a mother dragon, whose sons he has killed. In desperation he dashes into a smithy and the smiths lock the doors behind him. The scene emphasizes the importance of metal-working: the doors of the smithy are made of iron; as additional protection, the smiths may encircle the building with iron bands; they make a metal whip to thrash the dragon; and with red-hot tongs, straight from the forge, they seize her tongue when she licks her way through the doors. The second episode follows the first, and concerns harnessing the defeated dragon to a huge plough made in the smithy and ploughing a giant furrow with it from Kiev down to the sea.

Many of the narratives that contain this episode have an aetiological function, explaining the existence along the banks of the Dnepr and other parts of Ukraine of the so-called 'dragons' ramparts', tall earthworks that were probably erected as part of the line of defence against invaders from the steppes. In the tales about the south Russian and Ukrainian hero, Nikita the Tanner (Nikita Kozhemyaka), for example, the tanner makes a pact with the dragon to divide the earth between them, marking the boundary with the plough. Then he persuades the dragon to similarly divide the sea, and when the dragon has swum to the middle of the ocean, he kills and drowns it. In other variants the dragon is so thirsty it tries to drink the Dnepr dry and bursts. This ploughing motif also occurs in legends about the saints Kuzma and Demyan (Cosmas and Damianus), patron saints of smithing, or about the saints Boris and Gleb, accredited in folk beliefs with the miraculous making of the first plough.

Baba-Yaga

Unlike the *byliny*, the *skazki* abound in characters, objects and motifs that reflect an ancient period of man's existence when notions about the surrounding world were in the process of formation. For example, in the *skazki* the boundaries between humans and animals seem unclear. They may co-habit, producing prodigious heroes such as Ivan the Bear's Ear. Many characters share the attributes of humans and animals and shift effortlessly from one form to another, like Finist Bright Falcon, the frog-princess or the swan-maidens. Some animals are endowed with magical powers, the ability to speak or great wisdom, and may act as the hero's guide and companion. Some, like the grey wolf, the winged horse, the eagle or the huge Nogay-bird will transport the hero on their back as he passes from the world of humans into the realm of spirits. Others, again, may be fabulous prizes, like the firebird, one of the precious objects sought by the hero 'beyond thrice-nine lands'. In the *skazki* the most ordinary objects acquire magical potential: a ring contains the three kingdoms of bronze, silver and gold; a handkerchief, when thrown down, forms a lake or sea. In the course of his adventures the hero will come across many extraordinary characters: personified elements like Frost, Sun or Wind; mythical beings with superhuman gifts of hearing, sight, eating or drinking; the evil sorcerer Koshchei the Immortal, whose soul or death survives outside his body; and of course the ogress, Baba-Yaga.

Baba-Yaga is one of the best known yet least understood of the mythological figures encountered in Russian folk tales. A similar character may also be found in Germany and among the Greeks, Finns and Baltic peoples, while the East, South and West Slavs all know her (cf. the Czech *jezinka*). Her personality and function change from tale to tale and there are many different scholarly opinions about her origins and meaning. Adherents of the mythological school regarded her primarily as a celestial being, proposing that at least some of the tales about her were derived from myths about rain-clouds and thunderstorms. In Belorussia, for example, her progress across the skies was supposedly accompanied by thunder and lightning. By others she has been identified as mistress of the forest and the wild beasts that live there, and by others again as a goddess of the underworld, where she grows crops and herds her cattle. A more recent psychological approach has sought to connect her with a subconscious, if perverse, Slavonic perception of motherhood. She does, after all, eat small children!

One of the most popular theories regarding Baba-Yaga's primary role identifies her as guardian of the entrance to the world of the dead. While there is little evidence that she is a descendant of a pagan Slavonic goddess of death, as some have claimed, this theory is accepted in principle by many scholars today. Although originating in the nineteenth century, it is particularly associated with the work of the Russian folklorist Vladimir Propp, who also links Baba-Yaga with the priestly mentors of tribal societies who guided young men into adulthood through a process of symbolic death and resurrection.

Baba-Yaga's appearance and attributes

Characteristic of Baba-Yaga is that she is always old, grey-haired and repellent in appearance. She is referred to as 'Baba-Yaga bony leg', her skinny form suggestive of a skeleton. She may have iron teeth. Like an animal, she has a keen sense of smell, which enables her to detect the presence of a stranger. She is unquestionably female, though her large, slack breasts, which she flings over her shoulder when in pursuit of the hero, are unappetizing. Husbands or consorts play no part in her life, but she is the mother of daughters. Sometimes, the hero meets them transformed into a herd of mares by their mother. Rarely is Baba-Yaga the mother of sons, although among her horses there may also be a

Baba-Yaga riding with mortar and pestle through the forest. Illustration by I. Bilibin to the folk tale 'Vasilisa the Beautiful' (Moscow, 1965).

single 'mangy colt' who, paradoxically, turns out to be the fleetest horse of all. A further aspect of Baba-Yaga's position in a matriarchal world may be seen in the fact that she is often one of three sisters.

Baba-Yaga's mode of transport is idiosyncratic. She rides at great speed in a mortar, rowing herself along with a pestle and sweeping away her traces with a broom. Her arrival is announced by a stormy wind, reminding us that the wind is used as a vehicle by demonic beings. The large mortar and pestle, part of the common equipment of a peasant household and used for the crushing of grain into groats, may, along with the spinning, sewing or weaving with which Baba-Yaga is sometimes occupied, serve to illustrate the closeness of this extraordinary creature to the ordinariness of everyday rural life. Yet they undoubtedly also have some mythological significance. The mortar and pestle have erotic connotations in the metaphorical language of folklore. In songs and rites of the peasant wedding ceremony they denote the sexual act. It is in the tales where the hero, as a young man in search of a bride, asks Baba-Yaga for directions that she reveals her more positive side.

Vasilisa escapes from Baba-Yaga's house on its chicken legs, carrying the fiery skull to light her way. Illustration by I. Bilibin to the folk tale 'Vasilisa the Beautiful' (Moscow, 1965)

Baba-Yaga's house

In many ways Baba-Yaga's house, or *izbushka*, resembles a typical peasant dwelling. The few details we have of its interior and its contents, such as its traditional Russian stove, do not contradict this. Yet the house has features that are quite unique. Firstly, it stands 'upon a chicken's leg' or ' chicken legs'. This odd reference to the foundations of the house has never been satisfactorily explained. Propp suggested that the *izbushka* was a domesticated descendant of the zoomorphic tribal initiation huts in which neophytes were symbolically swallowed by the 'monster' in order to be 'regurgitated' later as adults. Others saw a reference to the chickens traditionally sacrificed in the foundations of a new building. Alternatively, this may be a visual image of a primitive building method, whereby a hut would be raised at its four corners on a pile of flat stones or even on untrimmed tree-trunks, with their roots still intact, as a protection against damp. This created the impression that the hut had legs and feet.

Baba-Yaga's house has other strange features. When the hero gives the command, '*Izbushka, izbushka*, turn your back to the forest and your front towards me', the house revolves upon its chicken's leg or legs. Sometimes, it is also described as being 'without windows, without doors'. Frequently, the house appears to be too small for its occupier, raising the idea that its dimensions are those of a coffin. The exterior of the *izba* is ghastly and threatening, reinforcing the perception of Baba-Yaga as the grim keeper of some ancient charnel house. In the *skazka* about Vasilisa the Beautiful the young heroine, sent by her wicked step-mother to fetch a light, approaches the house and sees that the palisade around the *izba* and its gate are made of human bones, while human skulls with glowing eyes serve as lanterns. Baba-Yaga's house is not easy to find. It is situated far away, remote from human habitation. It may be across a river of fire or a deep moat, on the shores of a great sea or in the midst of a muddy swamp. It may be underground. But most frequently it is in, or on the edge of, a dark impenetrable forest, that twilight zone of folk belief that humans enter at their peril to be tested by the creatures who dwell there.

Baba-Yaga, cruel antagonist and devourer of human flesh

In most of the tales in which she occurs Baba-Yaga is pitted against humans. When her territory is invaded, her house entered without her permission, or she is attacked or challenged in some way, she becomes a vengeful and cruel opponent. Typical are certain tales in which Baba-Yaga is the ruler of an underground realm. She travels with ease between her subterranean world and the world of humans, emerging from under a boulder or rising from below on a flat stone. Once arrived, she engages in ferocious combat with four brothers or companions living an isolated existence in a forest hut. Every day Baba-Yaga visits the hut (sometimes it is her own hut requisitioned by the young men), steals food, trounces the heroes and cuts a strip of flesh from their backs. When their leader follows Baba-Yaga underground, he finds further evidence of her cruelty in the old cowherd whom she has blinded, because his cattle strayed onto her land.

In some tales Baba-Yaga is portrayed as a tireless Amazon, capable of waging war for thirty years with the help of her army, magically generated by her tailors and cobblers. Almost every tale in which Baba-Yaga appears as a negative character contains some reference to her prodigious appetite: her house has a full larder; she pursues her victims with wide-open mouth or sticks out her tongue to catch them; she may be sharpening her teeth when the hero comes across her. This feature, too, links Baba-Yaga with the folk image of 'hungry' death.

In her least attractive manifestation she is a child-eating ogress, who catches her prey when they are vulnerable, having been left at home on their own or having wandered away into the forest. She will entice them by offering an apple, sharpen her tongue to imitate the mother's voice or call the boy, who is sailing his little boat on the river, with the song his mother uses. Once the child is locked up in her house, she intends to eat him or her. However, the child hero, like the adult, always has the cunning to outwit the ogress. He or she may persuade Baba-Yaga's daughters to sit on the frying pan, so that when the ogress returns home she eats her own offspring by mistake. In tales of this type Baba-Yaga is interchangeable with the ugly, northern type of *ved'ma*.

'Baba-Yaga fights the crocodile',
a satirical eighteenth-century
woodcut. Astride a pig, Catherine I
as Baba-Yaga attacks an implausible
'crocodile', Peter I. From Lubok:
russkie narodnye kartinki XVII-XIX
vv. *(Moscow, 1968).*

Many tales end with a terrifying chase, as Baba-Yaga, realizing that she has been outwitted and that her prey is escaping, often together with some precious object, endeavours to catch up with them in her pestle and mortar. She may use her sharp claws and teeth to tear a way through the trees and reeds impeding her headlong rush or wield her magic shield to send blasts of scorching fire after the escapees.

Baba-Yaga helps the hero

Although the frightening and negative aspects of Baba-Yaga tend to be emphasized, she is a character with a split personality and many tales reveal a positive side to her. In these situations the hero, less often the heroine, approaches Baba-Yaga for advice or help in solving some problem, avoiding danger or finding a wondrous object, such as the waters of life, the apples of youth or the lost person – bride, lover, sister – for whom they are searching. Baba-Yaga can give directions to the distant world of spirit-beings, 'beyond thrice-nine lands, in the thrice-ten kingdom', and can provide magical gifts to make the journey there easier: a ball that rolls in front of the hero showing him the way, a flying carpet, a towel that can turn into a bridge. In these tales Baba-Yaga's house and that of her three sisters, each one older and wiser than the next, are like toll-houses along the road to the other world. The hero can only pass further when he has convinced Baba-Yaga that he is not intimidated by her and knows how to negotiate with her. Two of the best-known tales of this type are 'The Frog-Princess' and 'The Feather of Finist Bright Falcon'. In the former Ivan-tsarevich, who has lost his shape-shifting wife by burning her frog-skin, is taught by Baba-Yaga how to find her again and keep her in human form. In the latter a young woman receives from Baba-Yaga a distaff of silver and gold, a silver dish and golden egg, and a golden sewing frame and needle, which allow her to rescue and win back her lover, Finist.

In the character of Baba-Yaga many of the dominant themes of Russian mythology come together: she rides on the wind, shares territory with the *leshii*, provides a link between the world of humans and spirit-beings, is connected with death, may be the mother of dragons and, in some tales, is a substitute for the *ved'ma*.

Conclusion

In this book it has been possible to indicate only a few of the more well-developed themes of Russian myth. Most significant among them are those concerned with a cult of the dead, an animistic view of nature and a belief in magic, all of which are interrelated. These retained their relevance down the ages, surviving to some extent even into the present century, while the official pagan deities of Kievan Rus quickly sank into oblivion.

In tracing these themes the intention has been to reveal something of the complex interrelationships that defined the Russians' traditional perception of their world. It was a world that scarcely recognized the rational boundaries between animate and inanimate, man and nature, the real and the supernatural, the living and the dead; a world in which every aspect of the mundane, from building a house to having a bath, from cooking one's porridge to getting married, was touched by an awareness of sacral dimensions in all their positive and negative manifestations. The unusual tenacity of this traditional world-view no doubt had many causes, including the sheer vastness of the Russia that lay beyond the centres of civilization. The relative lack of missionary zeal of the Orthodox Church compared with that of its Latin counterpart, in spite of its constant fulminations against the 'devilish' remnants of paganism, no doubt played an important role. The Christianization of Russia did not lead to the eradication of the old religion and the old myths and their replacement by the new. Rather, the old subsumed and transformed the new, producing that peculiar symbiosis of pagan and Christian that is sometimes referred to as 'folk Orthodoxy'.

Suggestions for Further Reading

Since this book covers many different aspects of folklore and ethnography the number of works on each topic is necessarily limited. For the early history and culture of Kievan Rus see: G. Vernadsky, *Kievan Russia*, New Haven, 1976; B.D. Grekov, *Kievan Russia*, Moscow, 1959; F. Vyncke, 'The religion of the Slavs', in C.J. Bleeker and G. Widengren (eds), *Historia religionum*, vol. 1, Leiden, 1969, and the section on pagan worship in M. Gimbutas, *The Slavs*, London, 1971; N. Andrew, 'Pagan and Christian elements in Old Russia', *Slavic Review*, vol. 21, no. 1, 1962, pp. 16–24. For the *Tale of Bygone Years* and excerpts from other relevant early texts see Serge A. Zenkovsky (ed.), *Medieval Russia's Epics, Chronicles and Tales*, New York, 1963. Two works – Yu. M. Sokolov, *Russian Folklore*, trans. C.R. Smith, Hartboro, USA, 1960 (Moscow, 1941) and D.K. Zelenin, *Russische (ostslavische) Volkskunde*, Berlin-Leipzig, 1927 – provide comprehensive introductions to Russian folklore and ethnography respectively. Commentary on paganism, witchcraft, magic, folk beliefs and mythological characters may be found in W.F. Ryan, *The Bathhouse at Midnight: Magic in Russia*, Stroud, 2000; L.J. Ivanits, *Russian Folk Belief*, New York-London, 1989; Felix J. Oinas, *Essays on Russian Folklore and Mythology*, Columbus, Ohio, 1985 (for discussion of spirits of place, sorcerers, demons, souls of the dead etc.); J.L. Perkowski, *The Darkling: A Treatise on Slavic Vampirism*, Columbus, Ohio, 1976. *The Songs of the Russian people*, London, 1872, by the 'mythologist' W.R.S. Ralston is a mine of information on pagan gods, spirits of place, funeral rites, Baba-Yaga, spells and much more. For folk tales and *byliny* see *Russian Fairy Tales*, collected by Aleksandr Afanasyev, trans. Norbert Guterman, London, 1976; W.R.S. Ralston, *Russian Folk Tales*, London, 1873, includes *legendy* and *bylichki*; *An Anthology of Russian Folk Epics*, trans. James Bailey and Tatyana Ivanova, Armonk, New York, and London, 1998, has excellent commentaries. Discussion of the folk-tale hero and the other world may be found in Maria-Gabriele Wosien, *The Russian Folk-Tale: Some Structural and Thematic Aspects*, Munich, 1969. Also of interest is Alex E. Alexander, *Bylina and Fairy Tale: The Origins of Russian Heroic Poetry*, The Hague, 1973.

Below is a very small selection of the works in Russian used in the preparation of this volume: F.D. Ryazanovskii, *Demonologiya v drevne-russkoi literature*, Moscow, 1915; N. Galkovskii, *Bor'ba khristianstva s ostatkami yazychestva v drevnei Rusi*, 2 vols, Kharkov, 1916; B.A. Rybakov, *Yazychestvo drevnei Rusi*, Moscow, 1987; S.A. Tokarev, *Religioznye verovaniya vostochnoslavyanskikh narodov*, Moscow-Leningrad, 1957; V.N. Ivanov and V.V. Toporov, *Issledovaniya v oblasti Slavyanskikh drevnostei*, Moscow, 1974: L.N. Maikov, *Velikorusskie zaklinaniya*, St Petersburg-Paris, 1992 (St Petersburg, 1862); E.V. Barsov, *Prichitaniya Severnogo Kraya*, 2 vols, Moscow, 1872; A.N. Afanasyev, *Narodnye russkie skazki*, 3 vols, Leningrad, 1936 (first published in 7 vols, Moscow 1855–63); *Narodnye russkie legendy*, Novosibirsk, 1990 (Moscow, 1859); *Poeticheskie vozzreniya slavyan na prirodu*, 3 vols, Moscow, 1865–6; S.V. Maksimov, *Nechistaya, nevedomaya i krestnaya sila*, St Petersburg, 1903: V. Dal, *O pover'yakh, sueveriyakh, i predrassudkakh russkogo naroda*, St Petersburg and Moscow, 1880; A.N. Sobolev, *Zagrobnyi mir po drevne-russkim predstavleniyam*, Sergiev-Posad, 1913; D.K. Zelenin, *Ocherki russkoi mifologii: vypusk 1, Umershie neestestvennoi smert'yu i rusalki*, Petrograd, 1916; E.V. Pomerantseva, *Mifologicheskie personazhi v russkom fol'klore*, Moscow, 1975; V. Ya. Propp, *Istoricheskie korni volshebnoi skazki*; N.V. Novikov, *Obrazy vostochnoslavyanskoi volshebnoi skazki*, Leningrad, 1974; *Slavyanskie drevnosti*, ed. N.I. Tolstoi, vols 1 and 2, Moscow 1995 and 1999.

Index